YOU WHO CROSS MY PATH

שמחת עניך

שמחת עיניך

תוך היפה הזה

:פ, י, כן

שממלאות

את חלל

עני

לפמלי

אגב קילי /

YOU WHO CROSS MY PATH

SELECTED POEMS BY EREZ BITTON

Translated from the Hebrew by Tsipi Keller
with an Introduction by Eli Hirsch

BOA Editions, Ltd. ◈ Rochester, NY ◈ 2015

Manufactured in the United States of America

First Edition
15 16 17 18 7 6 5 4 3 2 1

Publications by BOA Editions, Ltd.—a not-for-profit corporation under section 501 (c) (3) of the United States Internal Revenue Code—are made possible with funds from a variety of sources, including public funds from the New York State Council on the Arts, a state agency; the Literature Program of the National Endowment for the Arts; the County of Monroe, NY; the Lannan Foundation for support of the Lannan Translations Selection Series; the Mary S. Mulligan Charitable Trust; the Rochester Area Community Foundation; the Arts & Cultural Council for Greater Rochester; the Steeple-Jack Fund; the Ames-Amzalak Memorial Trust in memory of Henry Ames, Semon Amzalak and Dan Amzalak; and contributions from many individuals nationwide.

Cover Design: Daphne Morrissey
Cover Art: *Red Shoes* by Belinda Bryce
Interior Design and Composition: Richard Foerster
Manufacturing: McNaughton & Gunn
BOA Logo: Mirko

Library of Congress Cataloging-in-Publication Data

Biton, Erez, author.
[Poems. Selections. English]
You who cross my path : selected poems by Erez Bitton / translated from the Hebrew by Tsipi Keller ; with an Introduction by Eli Hirsch. — First edition.
pages cm — (Lannan Translations Selection Series) ISBN 978-1-938160-87-5 (paperback) — ISBN 978-1-938160-88-2 (e-book)
I. Keller, Tsipi, translator. II. Title.
PJ5054.B538A2 2015
892.41'6—dc23
2015019573

Lannan

BOA Editions, Ltd.
250 North Goodman Street, Suite 306
Rochester, NY 14607
www.boaeditions.org
A. Poulin, Jr., Founder (1938–1996)

Contents

from *Timbisert, A Moroccan Bird New and Selected Poems* (2009)

A Broken Nightingale

A Moroccan Offering

The Book of Na'na

Intercontinental Bird

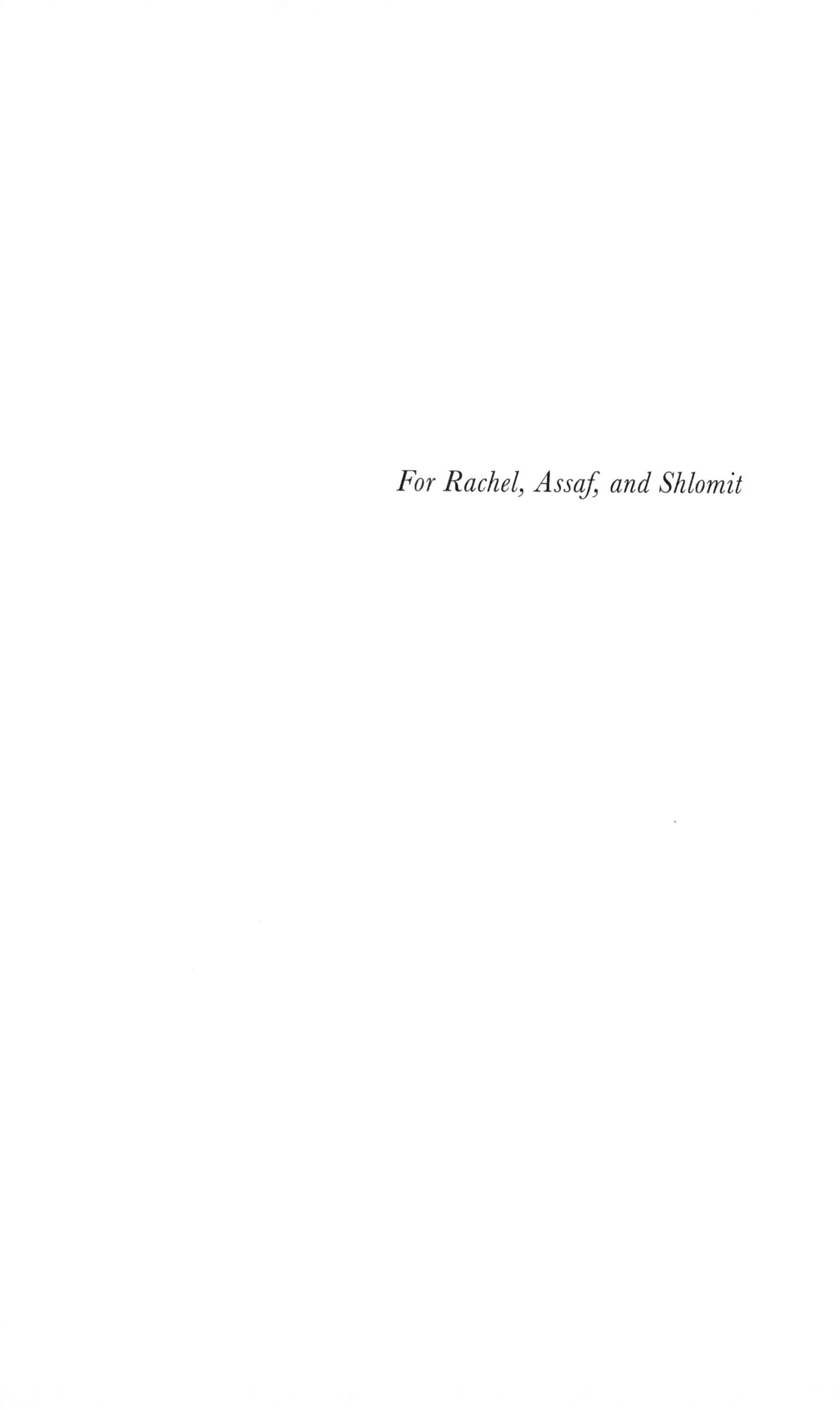

For Rachel, Assaf, and Shlomit

The Poetry of Erez Bitton

One cannot overstate the importance of Erez Bitton's poetry. At least one of the reasons for this is self-evident: Bitton is the dominant figure in the creation and development of a new and major tradition in the history of Hebrew poetry—the tradition of Mizrahi Israeli poetry—that is, poetry by Israelis of North African and Middle Eastern descent. Many consider him the founding father of this tradition, which dramatically expanded the scope of the biographical experience and cultural memory and became a vital part in the formation of contemporary Hebrew poetry during the last few decades. When Bitton first emerged as a poet, in the sixties and seventies, he introduced materials that, at the time, were deemed marginal or unworthy by the literary establishment. In fact, the tendency was to suppress and eradicate such materials as too "folkloristic," too Moroccan, too "oriental," but thanks to his great artistry, creating sharp and exact poems and redefining the direction of Hebrew poetry, such materials have since taken root in the contemporary scene as a matter of course. One is hard-pressed to name another Israeli poet who can claim such an achievement.

A few more introductory words are needed to shed light on the literary climate Bitton had to contend with in the sixties when Hebrew poetry was all but Ashkenazi. Ashkenazi in the sense that it was written exclusively by European Jews, and in the sense that it related—openly, and usually ideologically, by the veteran poets; indirectly and covertly by the younger poets—a very particular historical narrative: the story of Jewish emigration from Europe to Israel.

The literary drama at the time centered on the clash between two generations of Ashkenazi poets, a conflict that was expressed in a variety of aesthetic and ideological terms, but which, fundamentally, was based on different life experiences. On the one hand, the veteran poets were involved in, and bound to, the Zionist storyline, viewing the Holocaust, the Aliyah, and the revival of Statehood as major national events, worthy of a complex and an all-encompassing poetic expression—be it a lament, as in Uri Zvi Greenberg's *Streets of the River* (1951), or a heroic tale, as in Nathan Alterman's *City of the Dove* (1957). In contrast, the young poets turned their backs on those events, choosing instead to write poetry that was then classified as "personal," "nihilistic," or "existential," aiming to forge a new outlet for Hebrew poetry and Israeli society, and so liberate themselves from cultural traditions and hard-to-digest remembrances carried over from Europe. The tie to Europe did remain an essential focal point, shifting, however, from prewar Jewish-Eastern Europe—home to Zionism and most of the veteran poets—to postwar Western Europe, and the "West" in general, now adopted by the leadership of the young state as an ally and political model, and by a generation of young poets as a source of cultural inspiration.

The literary victory of the young generation was nearly absolute, obfuscating the Ashkenazi essence of Hebrew poetry and, at times, shrouding it altogether, and thus, in fact, grounding it more firmly. For the young poets, the negation of the Diaspora—namely, the Zionist principle of "making aliyah" (i.e., immigrating to Israel) and helping rebuild a new Hebrew-Israeli culture—no longer served as an ideological principle one could accept, doubt, or reject, but was now a de facto aspect of their life and culture. Indeed, the Diaspora, in its classical Zionist definition, no longer existed since European Jewry—the very Diaspora Zionism sought to counteract—was destroyed in the Holocaust, or vanished behind the Iron Curtain, and so, the quasi-denied Ashkenazi poetry of the fifties and sixties came into being, identified simply as "Israeli."

This resulted in two developments. First, the young Hebrew poetry of the time cultivated a self-image that was not explicitly articulated in real time—such an articulation would have undermined it—a self-image of a culture devoid of a significant Jewish past, floating in an eternal present wherein emigration, displacement, and a deep need to forget became an "existential" condition rather than a historical one—namely, the condition of modern man. The recent past, which, of course, did not disappear, served as a traumatic legacy, actual and yet denied: better not to recall it directly, but contain it within fables and sophisticated existential commentary.

Second, large segments of Israeli society, those who did not adopt this "modern" outlook, were viewed as "not (quite) Israeli." Included among those were Israeli Arabs; a great majority of Orthodox Jews, who sanctified other forms of historical memory; and, most notably, the immigrant and refugee population, who refused, or were unable, to give up their cultural heritage in favor of the dominant Ashkenazi culture with its perplexing insistence on amnesia.

It is important to note that such demands to forget, notwithstanding their presumed universal derivation, acted differently on the Ashkenazi and Mizrahi memory. The Ashkenazi memory had a solid and official expression in Israeli culture. It was fashioned by the poets of the previous generation and enshrined by the political establishment, playing a central role in the collective national mythos, the mythos of "The Holocaust and the Revival." The young Ashkenazi poets could therefore reference this memory, while also challenging and undermining it in their search for substitutes, and even shattering it to extract a truth that better suited their thinking and sensibilities. This approach—writing in the shadow of an official history that provided an identity one could challenge—had another advantage: it sat well with the young poets' vision of the modernist project: to crack or even break the collective "official language" of their parents and predecessors in order to build from its wreckage a more "authentic" speech, which, in the best modernist tradition, would be a sort of mosaic or collage, and thus reflect more accurately the broken and multifaceted consciousness of the individual.

The Mizrahi memory, on the other hand, and the wrenching migration that shaped it, found little expression in the official Israeli culture. The official mythos viewed the Mizrahi Jews as ancillary, as incidentals who had hitched a ride and joined the national journey of emigration and liberation whose cultural meanings originated in Europe. They were often viewed as phantoms of a Jewish past, remnants of a Diaspora, as not quite proper Israelis, namely, not modern Ashkenazim, not "Western."

From this it follows that, at the time, the challenge of young Mizrahi poets was entirely different from that of contemporary

Ashkenazi poets, and possibly more complex. There was no official Israeli language that adequately expressed their own and their parents' emigration memory. On the contrary: their legacy from the encounter between their parents and the official Israeli culture was mostly one of silence and silencing and, often, humiliation. Therefore, the stance of the inheritor-rebels—the inheritors of a language and culture they can mold anew—did not serve them. Indeed, as we will see, Bitton, who broke new ground, sounding the Mizrahi voice in Israeli poetry, evinced no such desire to break or to rip; the rift he was contending with was great enough already. He aimed for the opposite: not to crack or break an existing language, but to crack and break a silence. Not to rip, but to mend and to bind. And if the rift proved impossible to mend, then to find the exact, balanced, mended voice, healing and comforting, delineating the rift as clearly as possible.

This was the cultural climate Bitton had to forge his way through during his first years as a poet. He soon discovered that a significant part of his biographical and cultural memory, centered on his and his parents' emigration from North Africa—and absolutely essential for the realization of his poetic vocation—could not be expressed in the prevailing poetics. In effect, one may discern two layers of alienation or resistance Bitton had to confront. The mere fact of his wishing to recall his non-Israeli past was alien and menacing, as it touched upon the Diaspora with a great sense of commitment and longing, the same Jewish past that had to be negated. This wish was instantly denounced as "nostalgic," and even "atavistic," and in direct conflict with the modernist project that sought to replace the old and the no longer relevant cultural memories with a more "open," "secular," "progressive" cultural context.

At the same time, there was a deeper layer of alienation and resistance, targeting the concrete content of his memories wherein the Arab language held a commanding presence. Arabic presented a multilayered problem: it threatened not only the quasi-denied Ashkenazi poetry of the time—which, precisely because it was denied proved to be fragile and defensive—but also the Western modernist façade it was attempting to adopt. Moreover, it was identified with the language of the Arab-Palestinian enemy.

These focal points of alienation and resistance were not only external but also internal. Bitton had to struggle against the Ashkenazi literary establishment that rejected his poetry, but, even more so, against himself, namely, with the basic principles of the poetic language he had grown up in and had adopted within the framework of his creative explorations. His very first poems, from the sixties, were loyal to the prevalent poetics, poems he would later describe as "existential" and "universal." However, in the early seventies, as he began to discover in himself the rift he had experienced vis-à-vis his contemporary Ashkenazim, he came to realize that this rift, in fact, is the driving force of his poetry, and that he had no choice but to insist on a different poetics, a poetics that would not deny his Arab-Jewish-Moroccan memories of the "Diaspora"; a poetics that would refuse to translate the rupture of emigration into fables or tortured expositions about the loneliness of modern man, but would aim to present the rupture in its concrete details. This is how one of his most celebrated poems came into being, a poem that opened his first book, *A Moroccan Offering*, with the charged title "Preliminary Background Words":

> My mother my mother
> from a village of shrubs green of a different green.
> From a bird's nest producing milk sweeter than sweet.
> From a nightingale's cradle of a thousand Arabian nights.
>
> My mother my mother
> who staved off evil
> with her middle fingers
> with beating her chest
> on behalf of all mothers.
>
> My father my father
> who delved into worlds
> who sanctified the Sabbath with pure arak
> who was most practiced
> in synagogue traditions.

And I and I
having distanced myself
deep into my heart
would recite
when all were asleep
short Bach masses
deep into my heart
in Jewish-
Moroccan.

To this day, when I read this poem, a poem I've read to myself so many times, I'm overcome with emotion. I hear Bitton's voice pierce through the history of Israeli poetry, and Hebrew poetry as a whole, piercing through time and space, memory and forgetfulness, speech and silence, as he seeks to open new paths. First and foremost, this poem is a subtle cry of anguish, a hushed and yet reverberating lament, about the fate of Moroccan Jewish culture, about the fog of humiliation and forgetfulness his parents had sunk into in their new land. At the same time, it is a wakeup call Bitton addresses to himself and his Mizrahi kinsfolk, a call that invites them to break through the fog that had invaded their soul, but to do so honestly—without dimming the extent of the pain, but with the strength and love that such an act demands. The poem is also "preliminary background words" whose role it is to spell out for Bitton's readers, both Mizrahi and Ashkenazi, how deep the fog, and how long the journey to break through it. What is most ingenious here is that the poem, in its three facets, employs a delicate, internalized diction, words that convey inner distances and a yearning to bridge them, in a voice that is saturated, and yet balanced and clear.

There's a fair dose of irony here, both in the metaphor that ends the poem "short Bach masses / […] in Jewish- / Moroccan" (namely, Arabic), as well as in the description of the mother who emerges from "a nightingale's cradle of a thousand Arabian nights" and the father who "sanctified the Sabbath with pure arak." Still, the irony in "Preliminary Background Words," and in Bitton's poetry in general, is not deployed as an instrument of nullification or the splitting of meanings—a strategy we find in the Ashkenazi poetry of the time that sanctified the existential and emotional ambivalence of the "modern condition," focusing on the all-too-predictable futility of longing for love and meaning.

Conversely, Bitton's irony serves as a balancing act, or as a necessary brake to the emotional honesty and the assertive ideation of the poem; furthermore, it is a binding ingredient that holds together its clashing elements: the cry of anguish and lament, the call to rise, the spelling-out for those who may be in the dark, the protest and anger and, above all, the yearning, love, and succor—all fusing into one voice, fluid and precise. It is this unique, binding voice that is key to the great achievement of Bitton's work.

Another poem with a similar objective is "Zohra El Fassia" that tells the story of a celebrated singer in Morocco who was neglected and forgotten once she arrived in Israel. Bitton, in his function as a social worker, came to know her in the sixties, but wrote the poem in the seventies when he resolved to engage his Mizrahi memory and make it part of Israeli culture and poetry:

> Zohra El Fassia
> a singer at the court of King Muhammad the Fifth in Rabat,
> Morocco.
> It is said that when she sang
> soldiers drew knives
> to push through the crowds
> and touch the hem of her dress
> kiss her fingertips
> express their thanks with a rial coin.
> Zohra El Fassia.
> These days she can be found in Ashkelon,
> in the poor section of Atikot C,
> near the welfare office,
> the odor of leftover sardine tins
> on a wobbly three-legged table,
> splendid kingly rugs stacked on a Jewish Agency bed,
> and she, clad in a fading housecoat,
> lingers for hours before the mirror
> wearing cheap makeup,

and when she says: "Muhammad the Fifth, apple of our eyes"
it takes a moment before you understand.

Zohra El Fassia has a husky voice,
a pure heart, and eyes
awash with love.
Zohra El Fassia.

Here, too, we can identify the merging of a lament, of a need to remember and to remind, and of the spelling-out for those who are not in the know, combined in a poem that is "a husky voice, / a pure heart, and eyes / awash with love." Bitton does not hesitate to sharpen the tension between a past shrouded in a mythological fog, a fog born of forgetfulness and humiliation, and a wretched present. Additionally, Bitton constructs the tension in vocal and musical terms by placing, on opposing sides, the mythological, Orphic force of Zohra El Fassia's singing in the court of Muhammad the Fifth, in contrast to her husky and unintelligible voice in a poor neighborhood in Ashkelon. However, this sharp tension is drawn with great delicacy: it is Bitton's own voice that gives a loving and balanced expression to these two contrasting voices, without trying to simulate them, without favoring the one over the other, and without blurring the deep chasm between them. With great precision he seems to be hovering right above the fault line itself as he merges Zohra's two voices, underscoring the depths of the chasm, while hinting at a new, mended voice that may arise from them.

While Bitton is viewed by many other Mizrahi poets as a literary guide and pioneer, this should not deflect from the fact that his poetry is one of the critical milestones in Hebrew poetry in general. His singular voice played a central role in releasing Israeli poetry from the hypnotic, yet limiting, impact of the fifties and sixties—exemplified in the early poems by David Avidan, Yona Wallach, Nathan Zach, Dahlia Ravikovitch, and others—and setting it on a road of stirring explorations during the past few decades.

Three basic changes characterize this process and, in all three, Bitton's influence is clearly evident: relinquishing a worldview that champions solitude and alienation in favor of a more social, communal, or familial outlook; relinquishing the need or tendency to mold complex aesthetic and metaphysic masks in favor of an accessible poetry, committed to its biographical, ethnic, and political content; relinquishing somewhat the modernist-progressive project in order to renew the link to past traditions, including the cultural legacies of the Diaspora. In the poems collected in his first two books, *A Moroccan Offering* (1976) and *The Book of Na'na* (1979), one can easily identify the new directions Hebrew poetry would undertake in the eighties and nineties and even more so in the last two decades. But Bitton was there first, before eminent poets like Zach or Ravikovitch began to write a more direct and involved poetry, and before young poets, Mizrahi and non-Mizrahi, took steps in the new paths Bitton's poetry had opened for them.

Bitton's childhood was marked by displacement when he, aged six, and his parents left North Africa and immigrated to Israel. A few years later he experienced two further displacements: at the age of eleven he was blinded by a hand grenade he found in a field near his home, and spent the rest of his childhood in the Jerusalem School for the Blind (where his name was arbitrarily changed from Yaish to Erez*). Thus he went from light and sight to blindness and darkness, and from his parents' home in Lod to a school for the blind in Jerusalem. Therefore, when approaching Bitton's poetry, one is well advised to take into account this complex background of loss and displacement.

Up until the last decade, Bitton wrote very few poems that explicitly dealt with his blindness; in his first four collections one may find six or seven poems where blindness is the primary focus.

---

*In an interview, Bitton describes his arrival at the Jerusalem School for the Blind: "And Tova, the attendant, now stands and removes my clothes, and hands me corduroy pants with suspenders and a flannel shirt and tells me my code number in clothes: 70. She says to me: 'This name of yours, Yaish, what's that?' And before I have a chance to stutter something in response, she says: 'From now on we will call you Erez, it's a nice Hebrew name.'" Later in the interview, Bitton relates another pivotal moment at school: "In those days I was about twelve years old. It was Shabbat, all the kids sat on the benches in the sun, some reading a thick Braille book, others kicking around a can, and I stood up and declared: 'When I grow up I'll be a poet!' I felt it was a declaration of my vocation. A kind of joy washed over me."

No doubt, blindness had a crucial effect on his work, and one can find hints of this in his poetry, but Bitton's essential tendency as a poet was to downplay the blindness and concentrate on creating a literary space that would contain and possibly meld the rift of the displacement from North Africa and revive a memory that had been uprooted and silenced. However, in *Blindfolded Landscapes* (2013), Bitton's fifth volume, blindness is at the heart of the poems. In fact, a number of them are devoted to the poet's recollections of the time he spent at the Jerusalem School for the Blind, namely, to memories of a period that divides between a sensual childhood of light and motion, and an adulthood that allows him to express and relive those memories through literary means. One may say that Bitton's achievements in his first four collections, bridging the cultural gap, have paved the way for the fifth: bridging the gap between the sighted and the blind.

As is his way, Bitton cuts straight to the point, beginning with the title *Blindfolded Landscapes*, alluding to the primacy of sight and seeing, and to the difficulty of writing a poetry that is, per force, blindfolded. The language of poetry, like all human language, is essentially a language of sight, and one of the central issues addressed in the volume is the issue of the achievability of a poetry not based on seeing and sight, but a poetry that relies on old memories that have been exiled to a realm of darkness; moreover, the mapping of this darkness, or the re-mapping of life and poetry in this darkness, is the main drive of the poems in *Blindfolded Landscapes*.

Before discussing the poems themselves it may be advisable to dispel the aura of mystery surrounding blindness and concentrate on the distinctive character of life in the dark, and thus on the unique nature of Bitton's poems on blindness. One of the important lessons one takes away from reading the book is that the attempt to see in Bitton a mythological, Homer-like seer who sees more than the rest of us, is not only misguided but may also miss the point. This is not to say that Bitton "sees less." He doesn't see at all. He saw when he was a child, and then lost his sight. His great mastery is revealed not in his ability to see more, but in his exceptional honesty and originality which allow him to write a singular poetry—the poetry of the blind, faithful to his life experience and contending with a loss that cannot be denied.**

Additionally, the concept of "compensation" according to which the blind sharpens his other senses and so achieves a special "spiritual sight," also proves problematic when reading *Blindfolded Landscapes* because it is Bitton's poetic gift that allows him to provide his readers, be they blind or sighted, with words that bespeak life in darkness and enlighten us about the place of poetry in the interrelation between sight and other sensual and emotional facets in human life: a yearning heart, alert ears, exploring hands, and scouting feet. In his book, Bitton deploys these four languages—the language of the heart, the ear, the hand, and the foot—shared by both the blind and the seeing, and steers away from the myths about "inner sight" or "spiritual sight" which, in fact, originate in the mythology of the sighted.

The language of the heart is possibly the most fundamental language among Bitton's languages of blindness, and is palpable in the poems he writes to his loved ones among the seeing, his wife and sons in particular, as well as in the poems addressed to his dear ones among the blind, some of them friends from the Jerusalem School for the Blind. These poems, first and foremost, consider the circumstance of an intimate life together, both mentally and physically, of the sighted with the blind, and of the blind with the blind. And while Bitton writes to the seeing (as in "Treaty with the Elder Son," "Your Eyes," or "Not to See Granada"), where the language of the heart tends to be expressed through the complex encounter between the poet's blindness and the seeing eyes of the beloved, in his poems to his blind friends (as in "Families

---

**Bitton has said: "I've been asking myself many times: Who is this Bitton who was named Yaish, and today he is named Erez? Who would I have been had I not been wounded? I would probably have become an employee at the airport, raising a family and living in Lod. I wouldn't have become who I am. This is not to say that I am happy I became blind. There still lingers in me a deep longing for sight. I was a child of light, a child wherein colors vied for his eyes. Blindness is a massive, groping, dependent reality, but blindness transformed me from Yaish to Erez, to an inquisitive person, constantly contemplating and questioning everything."

at the Jerusalem School for the Blind") it is expressed through the meeting of bodies in the dark—a meeting of yearning in a space of mutual loneliness. It may be said that, differing from the other languages Bitton constructs in *Blindfolded Landscapes*, the language of the heart tends to involve the entire body, or to focus on his sightless eyes, blindfolded, as it were, and their intricate relation to the seeing eyes of the loved one.

The language of the ear or, more precisely, **the language of voices**, is elemental as well. Poetry is nearly always an intimate meeting of the visual and the vocal, seeing and hearing, imagery and musicality. And when the element of sight is taken away, the complementary element is necessarily emphasized. The language of voices typifies many of the poems devoted to Bitton's recollections from the School for the Blind (such as "Children at the Jerusalem School for the Blind," "Voices," "For Gvira"), stressing the ability of the voice to break through the darkness and loneliness and connect with many souls in a musical-emotional collective flow. It is possible that Bitton's unique facility in fashioning a balanced and comforting voice in his rupture poems is partially due to his keen sensitivity to the voices that break through the barriers of darkness that separate the blind from the blind and the blind from the sighted.

The language of the hand is also evident in the poems, notably in the poems "To Say Desert," dedicated to Yehuda Amichai, and "For Elisheva Kaplan"—a poem of love and praise for a music teacher who quit teaching music to devote her life to typing books in Braille: "You / who one day replaced delicate piano keys / with the hard keys of the Braille machine / callusing your fine hands, / and nights, page after page, book after book, / opened worlds for blind children." Both poems highlight the association of words/hands/fingers and their power to open worlds: a handshake substitutes words in the poem for Amichai, as Braille does in the poem for Elisheva Kaplan.

The language of the foot, though, is probably the most significant—the language related to walking, hopping, running, stumbling; to the guide dog, to the groping cane—and thus to the ground and its various covers: pavements, "broken and worn down" ("Sights"); tiles that innocently cover "the pudency of ashes" ("On Top of a Wall"); rugs and carpets, trees and fences that the sighted can climb (or avoid) and the blind stumble over.

The language of the foot is central in two momentous poems—"Sights" and "When I Was a Child of Light"—that relate Bitton's recollections as a seeing boy. And whereas "Sights" keeps pointing the sights downward, toward the feet, upon "the pavements of Lod" that are "acquainted with bare feet" and with "Mister ben Rabi / strolling upon them on the Sabbath / parading shiny shoes," the poem "When I Was a Child of Light" draws the eye in the opposite direction, that of the seeing boy who can run distances, climb, soar to the heights:

When I was a child of light
treetops urged me:
Climb, climb,
come cuddle with us in the heights
and all the fences
lower than me
lower down on the ground

When I was a child of light
distances drew me to them
with the speed
of a different time

The language of the foot is likewise central to the two poems that frame the book. In "Blindfolded Horses," which opens the collection, Bitton writes, "In every blind person / a galloping horse abides / aspiring to tear across / distances"; in "On Top of a Wall," which concludes the book, Bitton commemorates his childhood home, now in ruins, and ends with the lines, "and conjure for myself a past and a place / that had turned to dust." The language of the foot, then, serves to reveal the prime significance of blindness in Bitton's life, a spatial process of contraction and collapse, a process wherein the three-dimensional world of the sighted collapses into a disjointed relief of dark paths and winding streets, of ditches and ruins, of pits and hurdles. In this contraction, a dense and perplexing world is brought to life, as well as something supremely delicate, reserved, and attentive, in the way that Bitton holds the reader's hand and carefully guides him through the maze of blindness, teaching him a valuable lesson in the practice of groping and stumbling, darkness and dust. It is the same delicacy, reserve, and attentiveness with which he had held the reader's hand and led him, in the seventies, into the maze of rupture, suppression, and silencing that attended the emigration from North Africa to Israel. In the process, Erez Bitton endowed Hebrew poetry with a wise and exact voice: a voice that cuts into the loss and pain, while remaining loving and mending.

—Eli Hirsch
(Translated by Tsipi Keller)

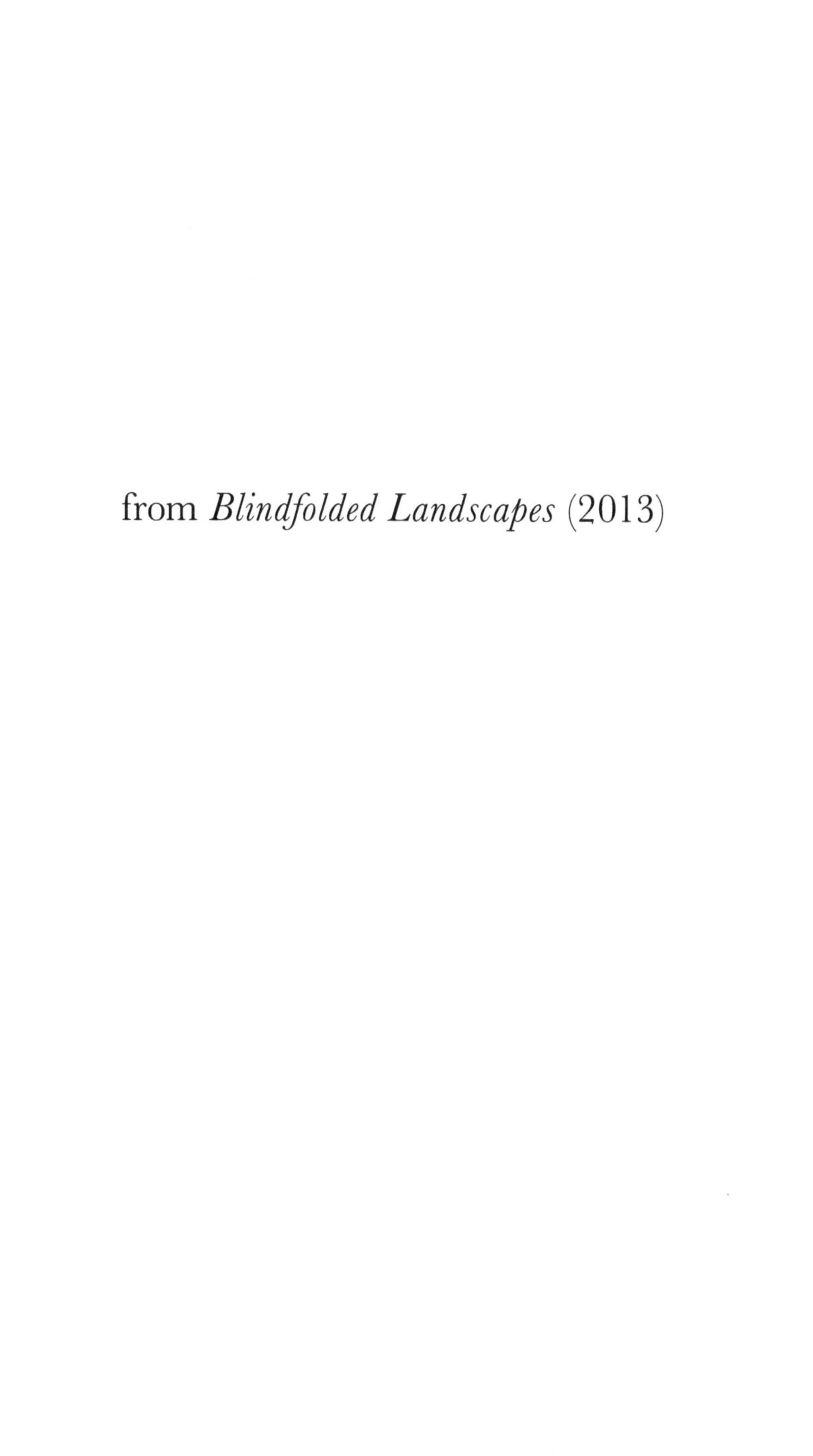

from *Blindfolded Landscapes* (2013)

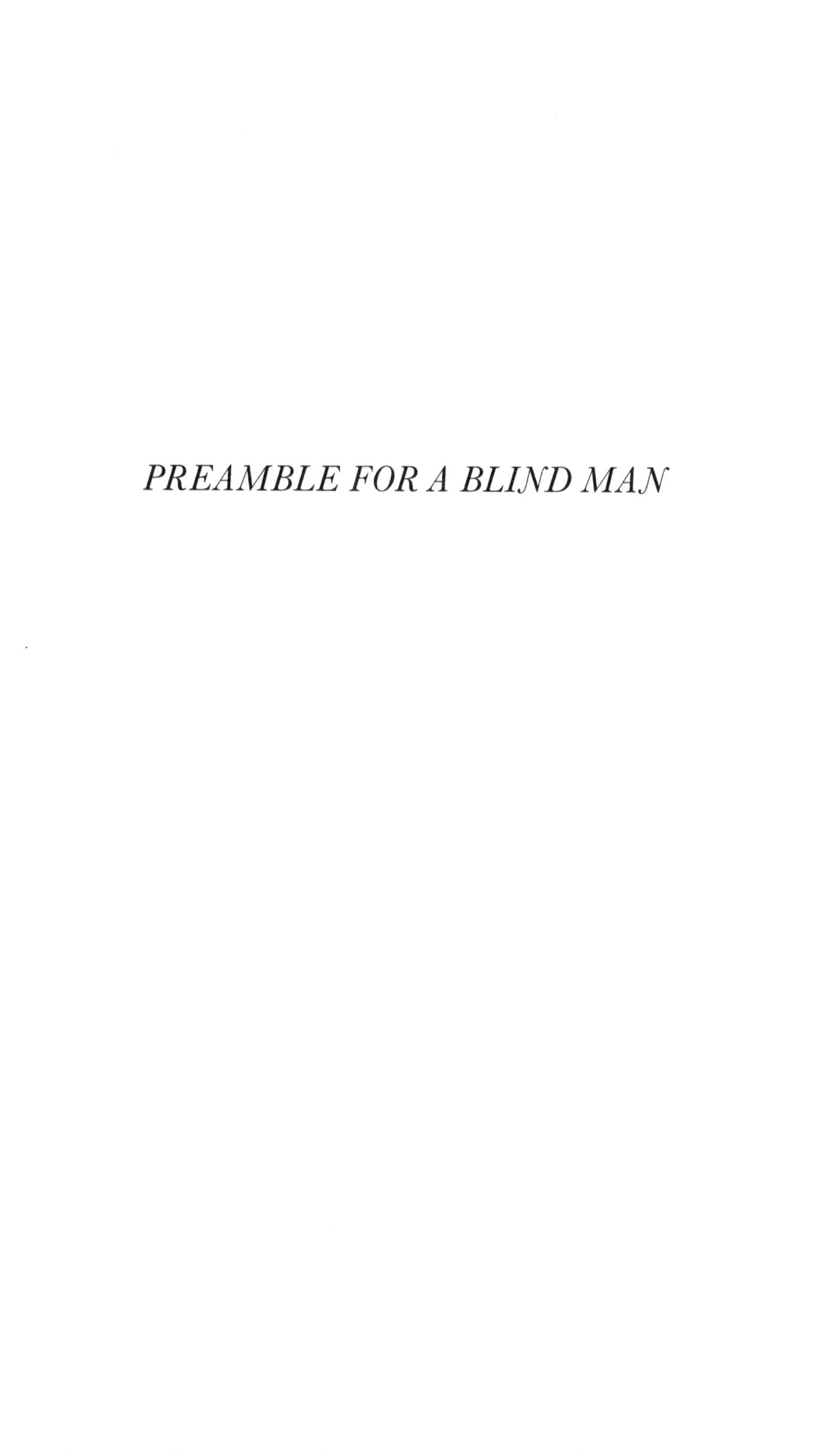

PREAMBLE FOR A BLIND MAN

Blindfolded Horses

In every blind person
a galloping horse abides
aspiring to tear across
distances

סוסים חבושי עיניים

בְּכָל אִישׁ עִוֵּר
נָטוּעַ סוּס דּוֹהֵר
הַשּׁוֹאֵף לְשַׁעֵט
לְמֶרְחַקִּים

The Dog and His Master

1.
The loyal dog will adopt his master's pace
step after step on his four legs
and if his master limps
the dog too will falter in his tread
descending a stair
foot stair foot
stair foot

so that his master doesn't stumble and fall
all the way to the bottom
to the flat landing

he will curb his ardor for boundless distances
will hold back the scent of virgin forests
ancient tales
the scent of the hunt beating within

2.
And what is a blind man to do
when his dog is suddenly ailing

he will cradle him in his arms
he will carry him in his hands
as if enfolding an infant
and will make his way
tottering on cracked pavements
walking into a tree
stumbling against a curb
and bring the dog to a vet
to the rightful rest
grace for grace
care for care

הכלב ואדוניו

א.

כִּי בְּקֶצֶב אֲדוֹנָיו יֵלֵךְ הַכֶּלֶב הַנֶּאֱמָן
צַעַד אַחַר צַעַד בְּאַרְבָּעוֹתָיו
וְכִי אֲדוֹנָיו יִצְלַע
גַּם הַכֶּלֶב יְגַמְגֵּם בַּהֲלִיכוֹתָיו
יֵרֵד מַדְרֵגָה
רֶגֶל וּמַדְרֵגָה רֶגֶל
מַדְרֵגָה רֶגֶל

שֶׁלֹּא יִמְעַד אֲדוֹנָיו
עַד תַּחְתִּיּוֹתָיו
וְעַד לַמִּשְׁטָח הַיָּשָׁר

יִכְבֹּשׁ תַּאֲוָתוֹ לְמֶרְחַקִּים בְּלִי גְּבוּל
יַעֲצֹר בְּחֻבּוֹ רֵיחַ יַעֲרוֹת עַד
עֲלִילוֹת קְדוּמִים
רֵיחַ צַיִד מַכֶּה מִבִּפְנִים

ב.

וּמַה יַּעֲשֶׂה אִישׁ עִוֵּר
שֶׁכַּלְבּוֹ חָלָה פִּתְאוֹם

יְעַרְסֵל אוֹתוֹ בְּיָדָיו
יִשָּׂא אוֹתוֹ עַל כַּפָּיו
כְּאוֹחֵז בְּעוֹלָל
יְגַשֵּׁשׁ דַּרְכּוֹ לְפָנָיו
עַל מִדְרָכוֹת שְׁבוּרוֹת
יְדַדֶּה, יִתָּקֵל בְּעֵץ
יִנָּגֵף בְּאֶבֶן שָׂפָה
יָבִיא אוֹתוֹ אֶל הָרוֹפֵא
אֶל הַמְּנוּחָה הַנְּכוֹנָה
חֶסֶד תַּחַת חֶסֶד
לִוּוּי תַּחַת לִוּוּי

he will recompense the dog
for his measured step
for his sense of smell
and for conjuring up for him
the taste of virgin forests
the sweeping charge of the hunt

יָשִׁיב לוֹ גְּמוּל
עַל הֲלִיכָתוֹ בְּצַעַד הַמָּדוּד
בָּרֵיחַ הַנָּכוֹן
עַל שֶׁהֵבִיא לְפָנָיו
טַעַם יַעֲרוֹת עַד
וּתְנוּפַת הַמִּתְפָּרְצִים אֶל הַצַּיִד

Poem of the Cane

When children cross the road with me
I tell them,
I'm a gentle man,
the cane in my hand
is not made to strike,
and when they leave me
down the winding street
only I remain
a child afraid of the cane

שיר המקל

כְּשֶׁהַיְלָדִים חוֹצִים אִתִּי אֶת הַכְּבִישׁ
אֲנִי אוֹמֵר לָהֶם,
אֲנִי אִישׁ רַכּוֹת,
הַמַּקֵּל שֶׁבְּיָדִי
לֹא בִּשְׁבִיל לְהַכּוֹת,
וּכְשֶׁהֵם עוֹזְבִים אוֹתִי
בָּרְחוֹב הַמִּתְעַקֵּל,
רַק אֲנִי נִשְׁאָר
יֶלֶד פּוֹחֵד מִן הַמַּקֵּל

This Summer

Will this summer once again come upon me
like a pest of grotesque beauty

a confounding abundance of scents and interactions
of promises that never amount to anything

and once again I will fall for a summer
that is a promise
that is a beguiling abundance

הַקַּיִץ הַזֶּה

הַאִם גַּם הַקַּיִץ הַזֶּה יָבוֹא עָלַי
כְּשִׁקּוּץ יֹפִי מְכֹעָר

שֶׁפַע מְתַעְתֵּעַ שֶׁל רֵיחוֹת וּנְגִיעוֹת
שֶׁל הַבְטָחוֹת שֶׁלְּעוֹלָם אֵין בָּהֶן מַמָּשׁ

וְשׁוּב אֶפֹּל אֶל קַיִץ
שֶׁהוּא הַבְטָחָה
שֶׁהוּא שֶׁפַע מְתַעְתֵּעַ

For the Algerian Poet Rabah Belamri[1]

1. The Algeria of Wars

We both came
from mothers wrapped in headscarves
like doves about to take flight
to leave behind hard lands

There
in the Algeria of wars
side by side they plod to the caves
to hide from the great uproars

You and I
knew how to seek out one another
with fine feelers
to reach one another
in a sightless friendship
predicated on purity of heart

2. When a Friend Becomes a Brother

When a friend becomes a brother
and he passes away
he does not abandon you
he comes to you with great compassion
he comes and goes
moving between the lines.

---

[1]Rabah Belamri (1946–1995). Algerian poet, essayist, novelist, and short-story writer, Belamri began losing his vision in 1962. During the last years of his life, he and Bitton became friends and often met in Paris and Tel Aviv. Belamri's book, *Shattered Vision*, is available in English (Holmes & Meier Publishers, 1995).

למשורר האלג'ירי רבאח בלעמרי

א. בְּאַלְגִ'יר שֶׁל הַמִּלְחָמוֹת

שְׁנֵינוּ בָּאנוּ
מֵאִמָּהוֹת עֲטוּפוֹת הַמִּטְפָּחוֹת
כְּמוֹ יוֹנִים הַנְּכוֹנוֹת לָעוּף
לְהִתְנַתֵּק מִן הָאֲדָמוֹת הַקָּשׁוֹת

שָׁם
בְּאַלְגִ'יר שֶׁל הַמִּלְחָמוֹת
זוֹ בְּצַד זוֹ, מְדַדּוֹת אֶל הַמְּעָרוֹת
לְהִסְתַּתֵּר מִן הַצְּעָקוֹת הַגְּדוֹלוֹת

אַתָּה וַאֲנִי
יָדַעְנוּ לְגַשֵּׁשׁ זֶה אֶל זֶה
בְּמְשׁוֹשִׁים דַּקִּים
לְהַגִּיעַ אִישׁ אֶל רֵעֵהוּ
בִּידִידוּת שֶׁאֵין בָּהּ רְאִיָּה
שֶׁהִיא עַל טָהֳרַת הַלֵּב

ב. כְּשֶׁחָבֵר נִהְיֶה אָח

כְּשֶׁחָבֵר נִהְיֶה אָח
וְהוּא מֵת
הוּא לֹא עוֹזֵב אוֹתְךָ,
הוּא בָּא עָלֶיךָ בְּרַחֲמִים רַבִּים,
הוּא יוֹצֵא וְנִכְנָס
וְעוֹבֵר בֵּין הַשּׁוּרוֹת.

Now, here,
you, Rabah Belamri,
are right beside me
quietly listening
as I speak with Mohammed Dib,[2]
your best loved poet
you wanted so much
to introduce to me
when you were still living.
See, I've always known you
to keep a promise

[2]Mohammed Dib (1920–2003). Prominent Algerian poet and novelist.

עַכְשָׁו, כָּאן,
אַתָּה, רַבַּאח בִּלְעַמְרִי,
פֹּה לְיָדִי
מַקְשִׁיב בְּשֶׁקֶט
אֵיךְ אֲנִי מְדַבֵּר
עִם גְּדוֹל מְשׁוֹרְרֶיךָ,
מַחְמוּד דַּרְוִישׁ,
שֶׁרָצִיתָ
לְהַכִּיר לִי כָּל כָּךְ
בְּחַיֶּיךָ
הִנֵּה יָדַעְתִּי
שֶׁאַתָּה תָּמִיד מְקַיֵּם הַבְטָחוֹת

To Say Desert[3]

For Yehuda Amichai

Your silent hand
drew for me
a desert oasis
green upon green.
As with connected vessels
a hand touching a hand
through your eyes
the greatness of the Word
was transmitted to me
as well as the wonder
of the burning bush.[4]

---

[3]After a joint reading in Arad, a town bordering the Negev and Judean Deserts, as Amichai and Bitton traveled to Jerusalem, Bitton asked Amichai to describe for him the essence of the desert as seen along the road. In response, Amichai held Bitton's hand for a few moments, saying nothing. Then Bitton said: "Now I understand." (Author's note.)

[4]Alludes to Exodus 3:2.

להגיד מִדבר

ליהודה עמיחי

יָדְךָ הַשּׁוֹתֶקֶת
סִרְטְטָה לְפָנַי
נְאוֹת מִדְבָּר
יָרֹק עַל יָרֹק.
כְּמוֹ בְּכֵלִים שְׁלוּבִים
יָד נוֹגַעַת בְּיָד
עָבְרוּ דֶּרֶךְ עֵינֶיךָ
אֵלַי
גְּדֻלַּת הַדִּבֵּר
וּפֶלֶא
הַסְּנֶה הַבּוֹעֵר.

Treaty with the Elder Son

When you learn
to play on the rim of my eyes
as if on familiar turf
banishing the fear of dark caves
I will teach you in return
how to walk with darkness
as you do with a friend
and you will not regret it,
son.

הסדר עם בן בכור

כְּשֶׁתִּלְמַד
לְשַׂחֵק עַל שְׂפַת עֵינַי
כְּמוֹ בְּמִגְרָשִׁים מֻכָּרִים
בְּלִי הַפַּחַד שֶׁל מְעָרוֹת אֲפֵלוֹת
אֲלַמֵּד אוֹתְךָ בִּתְמוּרָה
לְהִתְהַלֵּךְ עִם הַחֹשֶׁךְ
כְּמוֹ עִם יְדִידִים
וְלֹא תִּצְטַעֵר,
בְּנִי.

Late Learning

In order to resemble me
you are willing to adopt
the game of extinguished eyes
and like an unforeseen find
you hand the cane
to all the neighborhood kids
as if it were
a dove-sprouting wand.
Perhaps from you I will learn
to find a path
in my heavy-footed advance.

למידה מאוחרת

כְּדֵי לְהִדָּמוֹת אֵלַי
אַתָּה מוּכָן לְאַמֵּץ לְךָ
מִשְׂחָק שֶׁל עֵינַיִם כְּבוּיוֹת
וְאֶת הַמַּקֵּל אַתָּה מוֹסֵר מִיָּד לְיָד
לְכָל יַלְדֵי הַשְּׁכֵנִים
כְּמוֹ מְצִיאָה פִּתְאוֹמִית,
כְּמוֹ מַטֶּה שֶׁמַּפְרִיחַ יוֹנִים
מִמְּךָ אוּלַי אֶלְמַד
לִמְצֹא שְׁבִיל
בְּגִשּׁוּשֵׁי הַכְּבֵדִים.

You Who Cross My Path

You
who cross my path
and do not greet me
know that to me you do not exist
and therefore
when you come my way
say hello to me
and each one of you
will be my friend

העוברים על פניי

אַתֶּם
הָעוֹבְרִים עַל פָּנַי
וְאֵינְכֶם אוֹמְרִים לִי שָׁלוֹם
הֲרֵי אֵינְכֶם קַיָּמִים לְדִידִי
לָכֵן,
כְּשֶׁתַּחְלְפוּ לְפָנַי
אִמְרוּ לִי שָׁלוֹם
וְכָל אֶחָד מִכֶּם
יִהְיֶה יְדִידִי

ON THE WOUNDED NIGHT

My Father Gave the Neighbors

On the wounded night
my father gave the neighbors
a wine feast
and a variety of pastries
while my mother
unraveled both her eyes to the ravens.

And on tiptoe the neighborhood wives
come and go, lighting candles
to Rabbi Meir Baal HaNess[5]
and to Rabbi Shimon bar-Yochai.[6]

And I
feverish
toss and turn all night
soliciting my mother's eyes
to calm my father.

And the women continue
to come and go
to revive me
with nard and turmeric
until morning arrives
sealing the time
of darkness.

---

[5]Rabbi Meir Baal HaNess (Rabbi Meir the Miracle Master). Second-century sage, often quoted in the Mishna and the Talmud.

[6]Second-century sage, traditional author of the Kabbalistic work the *Zohar*.

אבי עשה משתה שכנים ביין

בַּלַּיְלָה הַפָּצוּעַ
אָבִי עָשָׂה מִשְׁתֵּה שְׁכֵנִים בְּיַיִן
וּבְמִינֵי מִגְדָּנוֹת.
וְאִלּוּ אִמִּי
פָּרְמָה שְׁתֵּי עֵינֶיהָ לָעוֹרְבִים.

וְהַשְּׁכֵנוֹת עַל בְּהוֹנוֹת
יוֹצְאוֹת וְנִכְנָסוֹת לְהַדְלִיק נֵרוֹת
לְרַבִּי מֵאִיר בַּעַל הַנֵּס
וּלְרַבִּי שִׁמְעוֹן בַּר יוֹחַאי.

וַאֲנִי
מִתְהַפֵּךְ כָּל הַלַּיְלָה
בְּדִמְדּוּמַי
לְשַׁדֵּל עֵינֵי אִמִּי
לְהָפִיס דַּעְתּוֹ שֶׁל אָבִי.

וְהַשְּׁכֵנוֹת בְּשֶׁלָּהֶן
יוֹצְאוֹת וְנִכְנָסוֹת
לְהָפִיחַ חַיִּים
בְּנֵרְדְּ וְכַרְכֹּם
וְעַד לַבֹּקֶר
גְּמַר חֲתִימָה
שֶׁל חֹשֶׁךְ.

Roll Call

They will stand upon me as if at roll call
                                                                        call
and I will have to raise my head from the pillow
in order to recall
                                                                        recall
they will try to appease me with the eyes of children
                                                                        children
and I will recall my graceless grins
                                                                        grins.

At that time
the fine words in my mouth
                                                                        mouth
will come knocking in my body
                                                                        body
and I will nestle against my weary aches
                                                                        aches.

At that time
the line of the horizon will shimmer
an airy smile of a cloud
and I will turn my face to the wall
                                                                        wall
and will not recall
                                                                        recall.

They will think that I make believe to spite
                                                                        spite
they've always believed that I do it to spite.

At that time
what will they find in me.

מסדר זיהוי

הֵם יַעַמְדוּ עָלַי כְּמוֹ בְּמִסְדַּר זִהוּי
זִהוּי
וַאֲנִי אֶצְטָרֵךְ לְהָרִים אֶת רֹאשִׁי מִן הַכַּר
כְּדֵי לְהַכִּיר
לְהַכִּיר
הֵם יְחַפְּשׂוּ לְפַיֵּס אוֹתִי בְּעֵינַיִם שֶׁל יְלָדִים
יְלָדִים
אָז אֶזָּכֵר בְּגִחוּכַי הַכְּבֵדִים
כְּבֵדִים.
אוֹתָהּ שָׁעָה
יָבוֹאוּ הַדְּבָרִים הַיָּפִים שֶׁבְּפִי
בְּפִי
לְהִדַּפֵּק עָלַי דֶּרֶךְ גּוּפִי
גּוּפִי
אָז אֶתְרַפֵּק עַל כְּאֵבֵי הָעֲיֵפִים
יָפִים
אוֹתָהּ שָׁעָה
קַו הָאֹפֶק יַבְהִיק
כְּמוֹ עַב חִיּוּךְ דַּקִּיק
אָז אַפְנֶה אֶת פָּנַי לַקִּיר
לַקִּיר
וְלֹא אַכִּיר
וְלֹא אַכִּיר.

הֵם יַחְשְׁבוּ שֶׁאֲנִי עוֹשֶׂה אֶת עַצְמִי כְּמוֹ לְהַכְעִיס
לְהַכְעִיס
הֵם כָּךְ תָּמִיד חָשְׁבוּ שֶׁאֲנִי עוֹשֶׂה כְּמוֹ לְהַכְעִיס

אוֹתָהּ שָׁעָה
מָה הֵם יִמְצְאוּ בִּי.

Sights

And here they appear before me
all the sights
hankering for eyes
I keep knocking on them
with the obstinacy
of one who's been branded

Here are the pavements of Lod
around the square of the central bus station
they're broken and worn down
yet well acquainted with bare feet
intimating races laughter and mischief
the trace of fear during tag games
and Mister ben Rabi
strolling upon them on the Sabbath
parading shiny shoes
or Mister Aron on his wagon
who got into fistfights here

This one and the other died
suffering trite and enduring afflictions
inside dilapidated homes
and memory comes and goes in me
bidden and unbidden
and I become a meeting place for a life
that was once chaotic and boisterous
and is now a deep silence
and pavements that no longer accommodate
the multiple interactions
the fleeting infatuations

מראות

וְהִנֵּה בָּאִים לְפָנַי
כָּל הַמַּרְאוֹת
הַמִּתְגַּעְגְּעִים לָעֵינַיִם
אֲבָל אֲנִי מִתְדַּפֵּק עֲלֵיהֶם
בְּעִקְּשׁוּת
שֶׁל מִי שֶׁנַּעֲשׂוּ בּוֹ קַעֲקוּעִים

הִנֵּה מִדְרְכוֹת לוֹד
סָבִיב לְכִכַּר הַתַּחֲנָה הַמֶּרְכָּזִית
שְׁבוּרוֹת וּמֻכּוֹת
אֲבָל מֻרְגָּלוֹת לַעֲקֵבִים יְחֵפִים
הַמַּזְכִּירוֹת עֲלִילוֹת רִיצָה בִּצְחוֹקִים
וּפַחַד קַל שֶׁל מְשַׂחֲקֵי תּוֹפֶסֶת
וְאָדוֹן בֶּן רַבִּי מְהַלֵּךְ עֲלֵיהֶן בְּשַׁבָּת
מַצִּיג לְעֵינֵי כֹּל
נַעֲלַיִם מַבְרִיקוֹת
אוֹ אָדוֹן אָרוֹן הָעֶגְלוֹן
שֶׁהָלַךְ כָּאן מַכּוֹת אֶגְרוֹף

וְגַם זֶה וְגַם זֶה
מֵתוּ בְּמַכְאוֹבִים קְטַנִּים מְמֻשָּׁכִים
בְּתוֹךְ בָּתִּים מַטִּים לִנְפֹּל
וְהַזִּכָּרוֹן יוֹצֵא וְנִכְנָס בִּי
קָרוּא וְלֹא קָרוּא
וַאֲנִי נַעֲשֶׂה מִפְגָּשׁ לַחַיִּים
שֶׁהָיוּ אָז הוֹמִים וּמְטַלְטְלִים
וְשֶׁהָפְכוּ לְקוֹל דְּמָמָה דַּקָּה
לַמִּדְרָכוֹת שֶׁאֵינָן מַכִּירוֹת יוֹתֵר
בְּשֶׁפַע הַנְּגִיעוֹת
וְהָאֲהָבוֹת הַחֲפוּזוֹת

When I Was a Child of Light

When I was a child of light
all the colors implored
my hidden pupils:
Open, open

Blue within blue
the colors vied
for distinction
as the evening sun peered at me—
rays
like two bright braids
of girls, a goad in hand,
leading a cow
in the town of Lod

When I was a child of light
treetops urged me:
Climb, climb,
come cuddle with us in the heights
and all the fences
lower than me
lower down on the ground

When I was a child of light
distances drew me to them
with the speed
of a different time

כשהייתי ילד של אור

כְּשֶׁהָיִיתִי יֶלֶד שֶׁל אוֹר
כָּל הַצְּבָעִים הִתְדַּפְּקוּ
פְּתַח, פְּתַח
אֶל אִישׁוֹנַי הַנִּכְמָרִים
הִתְחָרוּ לְהִתְפַּצֵּל
כָּחֹל בְּתוֹךְ כָּחֹל
וְהַשֶּׁמֶשׁ בָּעֶרֶב נִבְּטָה אֵלַי
קַרְנַיִם
כִּשְׁתֵּי צַמּוֹת בְּהִירוֹת
שֶׁל יְלָדוֹת הַמּוֹלִיכוֹת פָּרָה
עִם מַלְמָד בַּיָּד
בָּעִיר לֹד

כְּשֶׁהָיִיתִי יֶלֶד שֶׁל אוֹר
הַצַּמָּרוֹת דָּחֲקוּ בִּי
עֲלֵה, עֲלֵה
לְהִתְחַבֵּק אִתָּנוּ בַּגְּבָהִים
וְכָל הַגְּדֵרוֹת
נְמוּכוֹת מִמֶּנִּי
נָמוּךְ מִכָּל נָמוּךְ.
כְּשֶׁהָיִיתִי יֶלֶד שֶׁל אוֹר
הַמֶּרְחַקִּים
שֶׁאֲבוּ אוֹתִי אֲלֵיהֶם
בִּמְהִירוּת
שֶׁל זְמַן אַחֵר

With the Kids

If you strike your thigh
you'll instantly arrive
at Bnei Abid.[7]

That's what we, the fastest kids in the neighborhood, used to say.

Now
cross-eyed Swido Lechval
tries to placate me with flattery:
You were the fastest runner in the neighborhood,
and I don't tell him that one can discern his crossed eyes
even in his voice.
There are kids who hadn't known me before,
they sneak up on me and put a fluttering bird in my hand
and yet I don't anger,
a fluttering bird is a living heart
and I send her flying, a living heart to the skies.

But most often kids approach me with affection,
recalling adventures of walking upon tall narrow fences
or pitching a stone from a distance at a tree without missing,
and some of the older ones even place a coin in my palm.

When you grow up, my mother said to me,
you'll be like Mister Massoud, playing the oud,
gathering people around him
and bringing them joy.

---

[7]A neighborhood of new immigrants from Morocco in the town of Lod.

עם הילדים

אִם תַּכֶּה עַל הַשּׁוּק בַּיָּד
תַּגִּיעַ מִיָּד
לִשְׁכוּנַת בְּנֵי עְבִיד.

כָּךְ הָיִינוּ אוֹמְרִים אֲנַחְנוּ הַיְלָדִים הַמְּהִירִים שֶׁבָּרֹבַע.

עַכְשָׁו
עוֹמֵד עָלַי סְעִידוֹ לֶחֱוֵל - הַפּוּזֵל
וּמְפַיֵּס אוֹתִי בְּחֹנֶף:
אַתָּה הָיִיתָ הָרָץ הַמָּהִיר שֶׁבַּשְּׁכוּנָה,
וַאֲנִי אֵינִי אוֹמֵר לוֹ שֶׁאֶפְשָׁר לִרְאוֹת אֶת הַפְּזִילָה שֶׁלּוֹ
אֲפִלּוּ דֶּרֶךְ הַקּוֹל.
יֵשׁ יְלָדִים שֶׁלֹּא הִכִּירוּ אוֹתִי מִקֹּדֶם,
בָּאִים עָלַי בַּחֲשַׁאי וְנוֹתְנִים בְּיָדַי צִפּוֹר מְפַרְפֶּרֶת,
וַאֲנִי אֵינֶנִּי כּוֹעֵס,
צִפּוֹר מְפַרְפֶּרֶת הִיא לֵב חַי
אֲנִי מְשַׁלֵּחַ אוֹתָהּ לֵב חַי לַשָּׁמַיִם.
אֲבָל לָרֹב בָּאִים אֵלַי בְּחִבָּה,
מַזְכִּירִים עֲלִילוֹת הֲלִיכָה עַל גָּדֵר גְּבוֹהָה וְדַקָּה
אוֹ לְיַדּוֹת בָּעֵץ אֶבֶן מִמֶּרְחָק וְלֹא לְהַחְטִיא,
וְיֵשׁ מִן הַגְּדוֹלִים שֶׁגַּם נוֹתְנִים לִי מַטְבֵּעַ בְּיָדִי.
לִכְשֶׁתִּגְדַּל אָמְרָה לִי אִמִּי
תִּהְיֶה כְּמוֹ אָדוֹן מַסְעוּד, מְנַגֵּן בְּעוּד
וְיוֹשֵׁב וּמַקְהִיל אֲנָשִׁים
וּמְשַׂמֵּחַ אֲנָשִׁים.

Hoarse Rababa[8]

Why look to me for the flavor of a different time
for the juice of a large watermelon
for gleaming date pits
why look to me for a game of five hands
I, who had played the harp to seduce the Furies
and came back singed.
It is in vain now
that small tam-tam drums solicit fervent fingers from me
in vain the delights of summer thirstily tempt the pupils of my eyes
two broken ducts
now
my heart is dead to white bridal veils
to a large juicy watermelon.
Now
I'm a hoarse Rababa in a dark bosom.

---

[8]A one-string instrument Bedouins play, usually in the evening around the fire. (Author's note.)

רַבָּאבָּא צרודה

מָה אַתָּה מְחַפֵּשׂ בִּי חַד שֶׁל זְמַן אַחֵר
עֲסִיס אֲבַטִּיחַ גָּדוֹל
גַּלְעִינֵי תָּמָר מַבְהִיקִים
מָה אַתֶּם מְחַפְּשִׂים בִּי יָדַיִם לְמִשְׂחַק הֶחָמֵשׁ
אֲנִי שֶׁהָלַכְתִּי בְּנֵבֶל לְשַׁדֵּל אֶת הַפּוֹרִיּוֹת
חָזַרְתִּי חָרוּד.
לַשָּׁוְא עַכְשָׁו
תֻּפֵּי טַמְטַם קְטַנִּים מַזְמִינִים בִּי אֶצְבָּעוֹת חוֹשְׁקוֹת
לַשָּׁוְא חֶמְדַּת קַיִץ מְדַפֶּקֶת צְמֵאָה עַל אִישׁוֹנֵי עֵינַי
שְׁתֵּי שְׁקָתוֹת שְׁבוּרוֹת
עַכְשָׁו
לִבִּי מֵת לְהִינוֹמוֹת לְבָנוֹת
לַעֲסִיס אֲבַטִּיחַ גָּדוֹל.
עַכְשָׁו
אֲנִי רַבָּאבָּא צְרוּדָה בְּחֵיק שָׁחֹר.

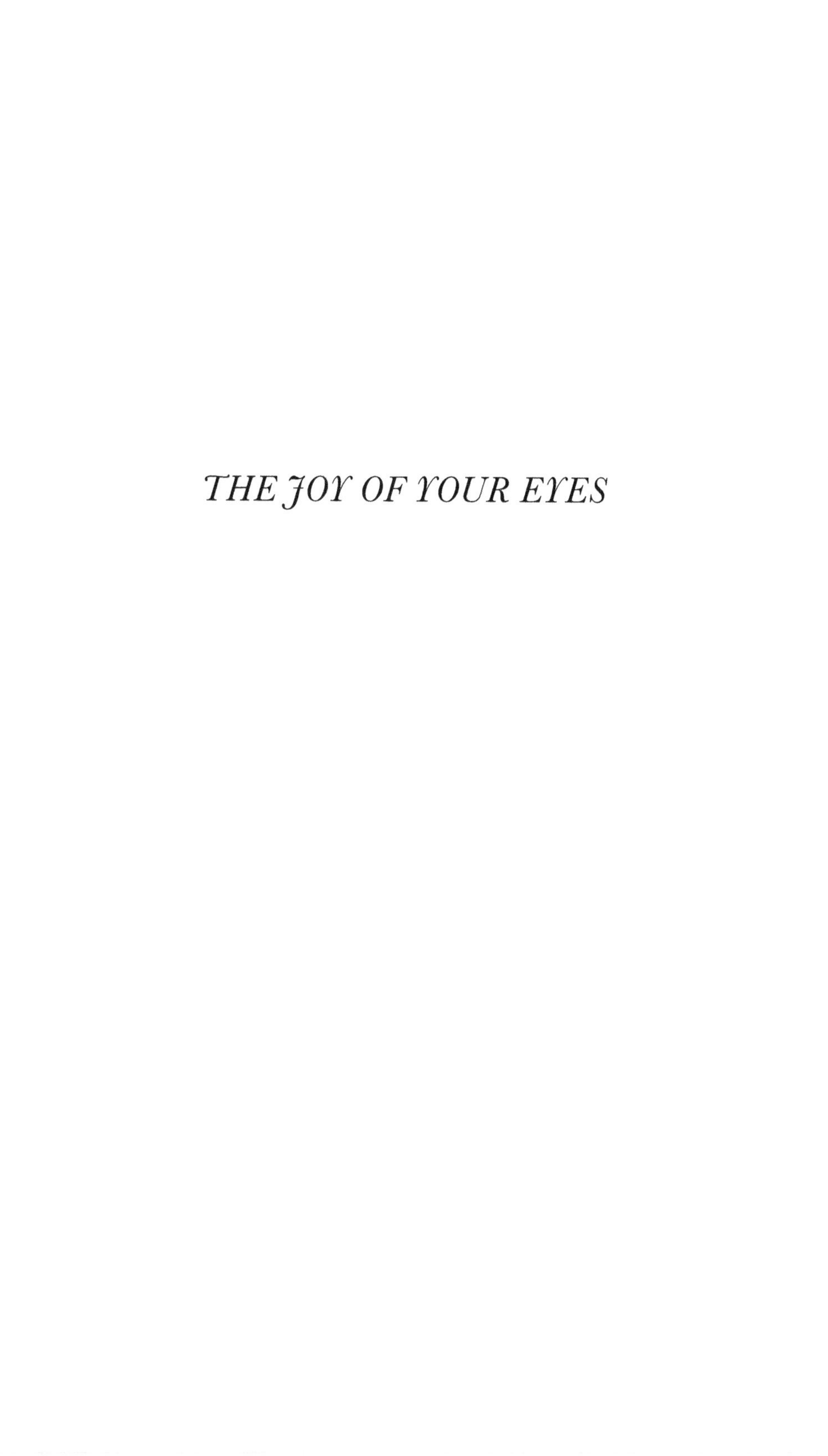

THE JOY OF YOUR EYES

Your Eyes

The joy of your eyes in this beautiful landscape
fills the cavity in my eyes.

And when we part

the joy of your eyes
alone
the cavity of my eyes
alone

עינייך

שִׂמְחַת עֵינַיִךְ בַּנּוֹף הַיָּפֶה הַזֶּה
הִיא שֶׁמְּמַלֵּאת אֶת חֲלַל עֵינַי.

וּכְשֶׁנִּפְרַדְנוּ

שִׂמְחַת עֵינַיִךְ
לְבַד
חֲלַל עֵינַי
לְבַד

More and More

You grow and become in me
more and more
and I too become in you
where do I begin
and where am I forgotten

I pour unto you
the upheavals of my life
you pour unto me
your beauty
the delight of your face
you clear before me all hindrance
faithful to the correct pace
the measured step
we're both joined in pain
you and I are made of two mysteries
one joy and two wounds

I will yet pour unto you infinite bliss
we'll engender offspring of beauty
of great manifestation

יותר ויותר

אַתְּ הוֹלֶכֶת וְנַעֲשֵׂית בִּי
יוֹתֵר וְיוֹתֵר
וְגַם אֲנִי נַעֲשֶׂה בָּךְ
אֵיפֹה אֲנִי מַתְחִיל
וְאֵיפֹה אֲנִי נִשְׁכָּח

אֲנִי מַעֲרֶה אֵלַיִךְ
אֶת תַּהְפּוּכוֹת חַיַּי
אַתְּ מַעֲרָה אֵלַי אֶת יָפְיֵךְ
אֶת כָּל חֶמְדַּת פָּנַיִךְ
אַתְּ מְיַשֶּׁרֶת הֲדוּרַי
נֶאֱמָנָה לַקֶּצֶב הַנָּכוֹן
בְּצַעַד הַמָּדוּד
שְׁנֵינוּ כְּאֵבִים שְׁלוּבִים
אַתְּ וַאֲנִי שְׁזוּרִים מִשְּׁתֵּי חִידוֹת
שִׂמְחָה אַחַת וּשְׁנֵי מַכְאוֹבִים

עוֹד אַעֲרֶה אֵלַיִךְ שְׂמָחוֹת אֵין קֵץ
נְקִים צֶאֱצָאִים שֶׁל יֹפִי
שֶׁל פֵּשֶׁר גָּדוֹל

Not to See Granada

In a paraphrase about your beauty

Let me quote Lorca talking about Granada:
A blind man must not
enter your gates, Granada,
for he will fail to grasp your beauty

I say to you:
This is how I miss out on your beauty
I live beside it as if beside a rumor
and you miss out on your beauty
and you miss out on living your own life
beside me

לא לראות את גרנדה

בְּפָרַפְרָזָה עַל יָפְיֵךְ

עַל דְּבָרָיו שֶׁל לוֹרְקָה לִגְרָנָדָה:
אַל לוֹ לְאִישׁ עִוֵּר
לָבוֹא בִּשְׁעָרַיִךְ גְּרָנָדָה
כִּי לֹא יוּכַל לָחוּשׁ אֶת יָפְיֵךְ

אֲנִי אוֹמֵר:
כָּךְ אֲנִי מַחְמִיץ אֶת יָפְיֵךְ
חַי לְיַד יָפְיֵךְ כְּמוֹ לְיַד שְׁמוּעָה
וְאַתְּ מַחְמִיצָה אֶת יָפְיֵךְ
וְאַתְּ מַחְמִיצָה אֶת חַיַּיִךְ
לְיָדִי

Forgetting Something in You

To part from you
is like leaving a hotel room
always leaving behind
an unmade bed
the drapes a bit drawn
half darkness and half light
and always always
forgetting something in you

לשכוח בָּךְ משהו

לַעֲזֹב אוֹתָךְ
זֶה כְּמוֹ לַעֲזֹב חֶדֶר בְּמָלוֹן.
תָּמִיד לְהַשְׁאִיר מִטָּה לֹא מְסֻדֶּרֶת
וִילָאוֹת קְצָת פְּתוּחִים
חֲצִי חֹשֶׁךְ וַחֲצִי אוֹר,
וְתָמִיד תָּמִיד
לִשְׁכֹּחַ בָּךְ מַשֶּׁהוּ

You and I

At your side I am
clear and lucid neat and coherent
serene rather than ruffled
still
I remain gnarled and occluded
perched on a brink

For, as you know,
with every casual contact
I am primed for the great stumble

אֲנִי וְאַתְּ

אֲנִי לְיָדֵךְ
נָהִיר וּבָרוּר וְסָדִיר וּמְפֻעֲנָח
חָלָק וְלֹא מְסֻקָּס
אֲבָל
אֲנִי חָסוּם וּמְחֻסְפָּס
וְעוֹמֵד עַל בְּלִימָה

וַהֲרֵי אַתְּ יוֹדַעַת
שֶׁבְּכָל נְגִיעָה קַלָּה
אֲנִי נָכוֹן לַמְּעִידָה הַגְּדוֹלָה.

Yesterday's Kiss

Our kiss yesterday evening
gave a special flavor to my morning coffee,
to the croissant,
and imbued the entire morning
with a beautiful hue.

נשיקת אתמול

הַנְּשִׁיקָה שֶׁלִּי אִתָּךְ אֶתְמוֹל בָּעֶרֶב
נָתְנָה טַעַם מְיֻחָד לַקָּפֶה שֶׁל הַבֹּקֶר,
לַקְּרוּאָסוֹן,
וְצָבְעָה בְּצֶבַע יָפֶה
אֶת כָּל הַבֹּקֶר הַזֶּה.

THE HOUSE OF PIANOS

Families at the Jerusalem School for the Blind

And we are children
at the Jerusalem School for the Blind,
seven of us take hold of a child
and say to him:
You will be our father,
and we say to her:
You will be our mother,
one child's body brushing against another
to gather warmth
under the guise of jostling,
generating families upon families,
calling out to a boy: "Father Shalom"
and to a girl: "Mother Shoshana"
and one girl I used to call: "My sister, my sister Rachel"
and one boy I used to call: "My brother, my brother Yossi"
this is how we spawned families of make-believe
and we are children
at the Jerusalem School for the Blind.

משפחות בבית חינוך עיוורים בירושלים

וַאֲנַחְנוּ יְלָדִים
בְּבֵית חִנּוּךְ עִוְרִים בִּירוּשָׁלַיִם,
תּוֹפְסִים שִׁבְעָה יְלָדִים בְּיֶלֶד אֶחָד
וְאוֹמְרִים לוֹ
תִּהְיֶה אַתָּה אָבִינוּ
וְאוֹמְרִים לָהּ
תִּהְיִי אַתְּ אִמֵּנוּ,
וְנִתְקָלִים גּוּף יֶלֶד בְּגוּף יֶלֶד
לֶאֱסֹף חֹם
בְּמַרְאִית עַיִן שֶׁל הִתְקָלוּת.
וְעוֹשִׂים מִשְׁפָּחוֹת מִשְׁפָּחוֹת
וְקוֹרְאִים לְיֶלֶד אֶחָד: "אַבָּא שָׁלוֹם"
וּלְיַלְדָּה אַחַת: "אִמָּא שׁוֹשַׁנָּה",
וּלְיַלְדָּה אַחַת הָיִיתִי קוֹרֵא: "אֲחוֹתִי אֲחוֹתִי רָחֵל"
וּלְיֶלֶד אֶחָד "אָחִי אָחִי יוֹסִי"
כָּךְ הָיִינוּ עוֹשִׂים מִשְׁפָּחוֹת כְּאִלּוּ
וַאֲנַחְנוּ יְלָדִים בְּבֵית חִנּוּךְ עִוְרִים בִּירוּשָׁלַיִם.

Sketching the Future at the Jerusalem School for the Blind

In a place
where the long lashes of summer girls
are a distant rumor

In a place
where an inviting smile in a face of delicate features
is an unfathomable algorithm

In a place
where blue is a guess
and red a cryptic formula

In that place
we would hold hands in the dark
hand on shoulder, hand on shoulder,
coming and going, coming and going
in long corridors
in the step
of fortune-diviners:
You're an oracle, I'm an oracle,
sketching the future

בְּבֵית חִנּוּךְ עִוְּרִים בִּירוּשָׁלַיִם מְסַרְטְטִים עֲתִידוֹת

בַּמָּקוֹם
בּוֹ רִיסִים אֲרֻכִּים שֶׁל נַעֲרוֹת קַיִץ
הֵם שְׁמוּעָה רְחוֹקָה

בַּמָּקוֹם
בּוֹ חִיּוּךְ מַזְמִין בְּתָוֵי פָּנִים עֲדִינִים
הוּא אַלְגּוֹרִיתְם סָתוּם

בַּמָּקוֹם
בּוֹ הַכָּחֹל הוּא נָחוּשׁ
וְהָאָדֹם נֻסְחָה לֹא מְפֻעֲנַחַת

בַּמָּקוֹם הַהוּא
הָיִינוּ לוֹחֲצִים יָדַיִם בַּחֹשֶׁךְ
יָד עַל כָּתֵף, יָד עַל כָּתֵף
הוֹלְכִים וְשָׁבִים, הוֹלְכִים וְשָׁבִים
בְּמִסְדְּרוֹנוֹת אֲרֻכִּים
בְּמִקְצָב
שֶׁל מְנַחֲשִׁים בָּאוֹב
אַתָּה אוֹרַקְל, אֲנִי אוֹרַקְל
מְסַרְטְטִים עֲתִידוֹת

Children at the Jerusalem School for the Blind

And we are children at the Jerusalem School for the Blind
diffident on tiptoe
pressing cheek to glass door
to listen to you playing the harp,
Ephraim Manofla.

Beyond alien hallways
like humming nightingales
dazzling a song blind.

You,
who harbored the promise of great symphonies of love,
what do you say now
as you eke out a living
with a broken mandolin
of three strings
at the central bus station in Tel Aviv.

ילדים בבית חינוך עיוורים בירושלים

וַאֲנַחְנוּ יְלָדִים בְּבֵית חִנּוּךְ עִוְרִים בִּירוּשָׁלַיִם
נֶחְבָּאִים בִּבְהוֹנוֹת
מַצְמִידִים לֶחִי לְדֶלֶת זְכוּכִית
לִשְׁמֹעַ אֶת נְגִינַת הַנֵּבֶל שֶׁלְּךָ,
אֶפְרַיִם מָנוֹפְלָה.

מֵעֵבֶר לִפְרוֹזְדוֹרִים מִתְנַכְּרִים
כְּמוֹ זְמִירִים הוֹמִים
מַכִּים שִׁיר בַּסַּנְוֵרִים.

אַתָּה
שֶׁהִבְטַחְתָּ סִימְפוֹנְיוֹת אַהֲבָה גְדוֹלוֹת,
מָה אַתָּה אוֹמֵר עַכְשָׁו
כְּשֶׁאַתָּה סוֹחֵט פְּרוּטָה
בְּמַנְדּוֹלִינָה שְׁבוּרָה
בַּת שְׁלוֹשָׁה מֵיתָרִים
בְּתַחֲנָה מֶרְכָּזִית בְּתֵל-אָבִיב.

Becoming a Weaver

At the Jerusalem School for the Blind
Mister Zvi, the school principal,
would introduce me to visitors
and say:
"This boy
when he grows up
we will make for him
one strap for the left shoulder
one strap for the right shoulder
and turn him into a weaver
who will weave rugs
for kings and princes."

I did not become a weaver
and yet
at times
during moments of grace
my poems turn into
small rugs
for all and sundry

להיות אורג

בְּבֵית חִנּוּךְ עִוְרִים בִּירוּשָׁלַיִם
הָיָה אָדוֹן צְבִי הַמְנַהֵל
מַצִּיג אוֹתִי
בִּפְנֵי הָאוֹרְחִים שֶׁל הַמּוֹסָד
וְאוֹמֵר:
"הַיֶּלֶד הַזֶּה
כְּשֶׁיִּגְדַּל
נַתְקִין לוֹ רְצוּעָה אַחַת עַל כֶּתֶף שְׂמֹאל
וּרְצוּעָה אַחַת עַל כֶּתֶף יָמִין
וְנַעֲשֶׂה אוֹתוֹ אוֹרֵג
וְיִהְיֶה עוֹשֶׂה שְׁטִיחִים
לִמְלָכִים וְלִנְסִיכִים."

אוֹרֵג לֹא נִהְיֵיתִי
אֲבָל
לִפְעָמִים
בִּרְגָעִים שֶׁל חֶסֶד
שִׁירַי נַעֲשִׂים מַרְבַדִּים קְטַנִּים
לְכָל אוֹרֵחַ וּלְכָל דִּכְפִין

The Child Sitting in Corners at the School for the Blind

At the School for the Blind
the child with the runny nose
would carve in his heart one great love
at the School for the Blind
the child with the runny nose
would devise in his heart
great feats and prospects

At the School for the Blind
the child would sit in corners
gathering with his remaining sight
last rays of light
to turn them into suns
in a time yet to come

At the School for the Blind
the child with the runny nose
would collect
echoes of sounds
to turn them into symphonies of love

בבית-חינוך עיוורים הילד היושב בפינות

בְּבֵית חִנּוּךְ עִוְּרִים
הָיָה הַיֶּלֶד נוֹטֵף-הָאַף
מְפַסֵּל בְּלִבּוֹ אַהֲבָה גְדוֹלָה,
בְּבֵית חִנּוּךְ עִוְּרִים
הָיָה הַיֶּלֶד נוֹטֵף-הָאַף
מְסַרְטֵט בְּנַפְשׁוֹ
עֲתִידוֹת וּגְדוֹלוֹת

בְּבֵית חִנּוּךְ עִוְּרִים
הָיָה הַיֶּלֶד
יוֹשֵׁב בַּפִּנּוֹת
אוֹסֵף בִּשְׁאֵרִית רְאִיָּתוֹ
קַרְנַיִם אַחֲרוֹנוֹת שֶׁל אוֹר
לַעֲשׂוֹת מֵהֶן שְׁמָשׁוֹת
לֶעָתִיד לָבוֹא

בְּבֵית חִנּוּךְ עִוְּרִים
הָיָה הַיֶּלֶד נוֹטֵף-הָאַף צוֹבֵר
הֵדִים שֶׁל קוֹל
לַעֲשׂוֹת מֵהֶם סִימְפוֹנְיוֹת אַהֲבָה

Voices

Night after night inconsolable voices
reveal
our helplessness
children children
across the street from "Ezrat Nashim Hospital"[9]

Is your voice
among the lost voices
that reach us in the evening
faint
exhausted
the cries of those tied to their beds
in "Ezrat Nashim Hospital"

And we, we have always yearned to hear your violin
the sounds your frenzied fingers
rendered so well
here at the School for the Blind
where all sounds are distinct
rising from cracks and corners

And even when you randomly
drew the small bow
dazzled we would stop
and stand still
united with all listeners
in the knowledge
that as soon as tomorrow
again you would attempt to jump off the roof
and again we would try to stop you

---

[9]A psychiatric hospital in Jerusalem.

קולות

עֶרֶב עֶרֶב קוֹלוֹת לֹא מְנֻחָמִים
מַסְגִּירִים
אֶת חֹסֶר הָאוֹנִים שֶׁלָּנוּ
יְלָדִים יְלָדִים
אֶל מוּל בֵּית הַחוֹלִים "עֶזְרַת נָשִׁים"
הַאִם קוֹלְךָ שָׁזוּר
בַּקּוֹלוֹת הָאֲבוּדִים
הַמַּגִּיעִים אֵלֵינוּ בָּעֶרֶב
קְלוּשִׁים
בִּשְׁאֵרִית כּוֹחָם
שֶׁמְּקוֹרָם בְּזַעֲקוֹת הַנִּכְפָּתִים אֶל הַמִּטּוֹת
בְּבֵית הַחוֹלִים "עֶזְרַת נָשִׁים"
וַאֲנַחְנוּ יְחַלְנוּ לְקוֹל הַכִּנּוֹר שֶׁלְּךָ
שֶׁיָּדַעְתָּ כָּל כָּךְ
לְהָפִיק מֵאֶצְבָּעוֹת טְרוּפוֹת תְּזָזִית
כָּאן בְּבֵית חִנּוּךְ עִוְּרִים
כָּל הַקּוֹלוֹת גְּלוּיִים
בָּאִים מֵחֲרַכִּים וּמִן הַפִּנּוֹת
וְגַם כְּשֶׁהָיִיתָ מוֹשֵׁךְ בְּאַקְרַאי
בַּקֶּשֶׁת הַקְּטַנָּה
הָיִינוּ טְרוּפֵי דַּעַת עוֹמְדִים
בַּאֲשֶׁר הָיִינוּ
וְיָדַעְנוּ בִּידִיעָה מְשֻׁתֶּפֶת
שֶׁל כָּל הַשּׁוֹמְעִים
שֶׁכְּבָר מָחָר
תְּנַסֶּה שׁוּב לִקְפֹּץ מִן הַגַּג
וְשׁוּב נְנַסֶּה לַעֲצֹר בְּךָ

holding onto your clothing
so that you don't depart from yourself
so we can entreat you
not to take to the air
with your violin

You who transformed stale air
into the breath of mountains
into the scents of distant gardens
still remain unsolved
and we are unsolved
the loop of sounds
like the loop of the secret joy
of hearing again and again
the violin play
in the basements and the attics
of the house of pianos

וְלִתְפֹּס בְּבִגְדְךָ
כְּדֵי שֶׁלֹּא תֵּצֵא מֵעַצְמְךָ
כְּדֵי לַעֲתֹר בְּךָ
שֶׁלֹּא תִּדְאֶה עִם כִּנּוֹרְךָ

אַתָּה שֶׁהָיִיתָ הוֹפֵךְ אֲוִיר סָתוּם
לְנִשְׁמַת הָרִים
לְרֵיחוֹת גַּנִּים רְחוֹקִים.
אַתָּה נוֹתַרְתָּ לֹא פָּתוּר
וַאֲנַחְנוּ לֹא פְּתוּרִים
פְּקַעַת הַקּוֹלוֹת
כִּפְקַעַת הַשִּׂמְחָה הַנִּכְלֶמֶת
לִשְׁמֹעַ שׁוּב וָשׁוּב
אֶת נְגִינַת הַכִּנּוֹר
בַּמַּרְתְּפִים וּבַעֲלִיּוֹת הַגַּג
שֶׁל בֵּית הַפְּסַנְתֵּרִים

For Gvira[10]

You who gathered us each morning
in a small room
as if gathering abandoned eggs
you who knew how to listen
who knew how to disentangle in us
land mines of loneliness
land mines of the quiet despair budding in children
asleep in their beds
bereft of a caressing hand
yearning morning after morning
to hear your treading footsteps
approaching the door
to listen to your healing smile
to your soft voice filling us with joy
from head to toe
as we chased away from within
the confusion
the fear
of those who feel desolate
when no one is near

---

[10]Name of a female teacher at the School for the Blind.

לגבירה

שֶׁאָסַפְתְּ אוֹתָנוּ מִדֵּי בֹּקֶר
כְּאֶסֹף בֵּיצִים עֲזוּבוֹת
בְּתוֹךְ חֶדֶר קָטָן
שֶׁיָּדַעְתְּ לְהַקְשִׁיב
שֶׁיָּדַעְתְּ לְפָרֵק בָּנוּ
מוֹקְשִׁים שֶׁל בְּדִידוּת
שֶׁל יֵאוּשׁ שָׁקֵט הַנּוֹבֵט בַּיְלָדִים
הַיְשֵׁנִים בְּמִטּוֹתֵיהֶם
לְלֹא יָד מְלַטֶּפֶת
שֶׁהָיִינוּ כְּמֵהִים בֹּקֶר בֹּקֶר
לִשְׁמֹעַ אֶת צַעֲדַיִךְ הַמְדַשְׁדְּשִׁים
הַמִּתְקָרְבִים אֶל הַדֶּלֶת
וּלְהַקְשִׁיב לְחִיּוּכֵךְ הַמְרַפֵּא
לְקוֹלֵךְ הָרַךְ הַמְהַלֵּךְ בָּנוּ שִׂמְחָה
מִקָּצֶה עַד קָצֶה
וַאֲנַחְנוּ מְגָרְשִׁים מִתּוֹכֵנוּ
אֶת הַמְּבוּכָה
אֶת הַפַּחַד
שֶׁל מִי שֶׁנִּקְלַע לְחֹסֶר אוֹנִים
בְּאֵין אִישׁ

Mommy Wrap for Me

For N.B., my friend from the School for the Blind

Mommy, wrap for me
a small egg sandwich
that you know I love,
the blind child whispered
through the keyhole
in the room where his mother
had locked him up
to hide him from her guests

And the blind child
listened to the clatter of glasses and dishes
and to the ring of laughter
throughout the house

לפפי לי אימא

לחברי נ"ב מבית-חינוך עיוורים בירושלים

לַפְּפִי לִי אִמָּא
לֶחֶם קָטָן עִם הַבֵּיצָה
שֶׁאַתְּ יוֹדַעַת
שֶׁאֲנִי אוֹהֵב
לָחַשׁ הַיֶּלֶד הָעִוֵּר
דֶּרֶךְ חוֹר הַמַּנְעוּל
מִן הַחֶדֶר
בּוֹ סָגְרָה אוֹתוֹ אִמּוֹ
לְהַחְבִּיא אוֹתוֹ מִפְּנֵי הָאוֹרְחִים

וְהַיֶּלֶד הָעִוֵּר
שָׁמַע אֶת קִשְׁקוּשׁ הַצַּלָּחוֹת וְהַכּוֹסוֹת
וְאֶת הַצְּחוֹק בְּכָל הַבַּיִת

Yom Kippur at the School for the Blind

Said Mister Shvili the *gabbai*[11] to Mister Cohen:
Here is a day to attend to your soul
attend to the soul of the people
speak in the name of the people
make use of speech
call out and howl
put your soul
and the souls of these people
in the language
these people forged in solitude
forged in fire.
And Mister Cohen, a blind man,
limps on his hip,
all his days like blank pages,
he hobbles with his wife
from day to day.
And we are children
separated from our parents
and their daily hardships
in a town or in a village,
we replace solitude with prayer,
and Mister Cohen, the faithful emissary,
drains sorrows and paves the way
between us and veiled hopes,
his prayer transforming the pain
of solitude into bashful beauty.
And we know that like a shimmering butterfly
drawn to the light
Mister Cohen too will give all that he has,

---

[11]Also known as the *shamash*. A person of various administrative duties in a synagogue. The synagogue at the School for the Blind also served as a community synagogue for several neighborhoods in Jerusalem. (Author's note.)

יום הכיפורים בבית חינוך עיוורים בירושלים

אָמַר אָדוֹן שְׁוִילִי הַגַּבַּאי לְאָדוֹן כֹּהֵן
הִנֵּה לְךָ יוֹם, עֲשֵׂה בּוֹ נֶפֶשׁ
עֲשֵׂה נֶפֶשׁ לָאֲנָשִׁים
דַּבֵּר בְּשֵׁם הָאֲנָשִׁים
עֲשֵׂה שִׁמּוּשׁ בְּכָל הַשָּׂפָה
קְרָא בְּקוֹל וּזְעַק
תֵּן נַפְשְׁךָ בַּשָּׂפָה
תֵּן נַפְשָׁם
וְהָאֲנָשִׁים הָאֵלֶּה
יְצוּקִים מִבְּדִידוּת צְרוּפָה
יְצוּקִים מִשְׂרֵפָה.
וְאָדוֹן כֹּהֵן אִישׁ עִוֵּר,
צוֹלֵעַ עַל יְרֵכוֹ,
שֶׁכָּל יָמָיו כְּמוֹ דַּפִּים רֵיקִים,
מְדַדֶּה עִם אִשְׁתּוֹ
לְהַעֲבִיר יוֹם וְעוֹד יוֹם.
וַאֲנַחְנוּ יְלָדִים
עֲזוּבִים מֵהוֹרֵינוּ
הַנְּתוּנִים בִּמְצוּקָתָם,
אֶחָד בָּעִיר וְאֶחָד בַּכְּפָר
וַאֲנַחְנוּ מְמִירִים
בְּדִידוּת בִּתְפִלָּה,
וְאָדוֹן כֹּהֵן, הַמְתַוֵּךְ הַנֶּאֱמָן
מְנַקֵּז צַעַר, מְפַלֵּס דֶּרֶךְ
בֵּינֵינוּ לְבֵין תִּקְוָה נַעֲלָמָה.
בִּתְפִלָּתוֹ הָיָה הוֹפֵךְ
אֶת צַעַר הַבְּדִידוּת לְיֹפִי נִכְלָם.
וַאֲנַחְנוּ יוֹדְעִים, שֶׁכְּמוֹ פַּרְפָּר כָּסוּף,
הַמֵּיטִיב לָצֵאת אֶל הָאוֹר,
גַּם אָדוֹן כֹּהֵן יִתֵּן אֶת כָּל כֻּלּוֹ

his entire being,
and we know that
at the end of the day
with the blowing of the shofar
Mister Cohen yet again
will limp on his hip
toward his home
at the edge of the neighborhood
where together with his blind spouse
he will live day to day
through days of blank pages
until Yom Kippur comes around again.

וְאֶת כָּל מְאוֹדוֹ
וַאֲנַחְנוּ יוֹדְעִים
כִּי עִם תְּקִיעַת הַשּׁוֹפָר
בְּסוֹף הַיּוֹם
שׁוּב יְדַדֶּה אָדוֹן כֹּהֵן
צוֹלֵעַ עַל יְרֵכוֹ
אֶל בֵּיתוֹ בִּקְצֵה הָרֹבַע
שָׁם
יַחַד עִם אִשְׁתּוֹ הָעִוֶּרֶת
יַעֲבִיר עוֹד יוֹם וְעוֹד יוֹם
בְּיָמִים שֶׁהֵם דַּפִּים רֵיקִים
עַד לְיוֹם הַכִּפּוּרִים הַבָּא.

For Elisheva Kaplan[12]

You
who one day replaced delicate piano keys
with the hard keys of the Braille machine
callusing your fine hands,
and nights, page after page, book after book,
opened worlds for blind children

Here is De Amicis's novel *Heart*
here are Tarzan's wild leaps from tree to tree
and here is *The Last of the Mohicans*
battling and striking the white enemy,
and kids whose world is circumscribed
sharpened their sense of touch
stealthily traversing dots on embossed paper
discovering distant lands.
This is how they got to touch the world's features
deciphering codes enclosed in hermetic letters
summer after summer in unknown continents

What does such a reputable lady
from the Rehavia neighborhood in Jerusalem
share with a blind child
knocking on the world's door,
to compel her one day to replace
delicate piano keys
and callus her fingers striking
the hard keys of a Braille machine
and so granting key after key
to the world's gate

---

[12]A children's piano teacher in the 1950s, Elisheva Kaplan quit teaching and devoted herself to typing text books, using the Braille system, for the children at the Jerusalem School for the Blind. (Author's note.)

שיר לאלישבע קפלן

אַתְּ,
שֶׁיּוֹם אֶחָד הֵמַרְתְּ קְלִידִים עֲדִינֵי מַגָּע
שֶׁל פְּסַנְתֵּר לְנִקִישׁוֹת נֻקְשׁוֹת שֶׁל מְכוֹנַת הַבַּרְזֶל
וְהָפַכְתְּ אֶת יָדַיִךְ הָאֲצִילוֹת לְאֶצְבָּעוֹת מְסֻקָּסוֹת,
וּבַלֵּילוֹת, דַּף וְעוֹד דַּף, סֵפֶר וְעוֹד סֵפֶר
פָּתַחְתְּ עוֹלָמוֹת לִילָדִים עִוְּרִים

הִנֵּה סֵפֶר הַלֵּב שֶׁל דֶ'אָמִיצִ'יס,
הִנֵּה זִנּוּקִים פִּרְאִיִּים שֶׁל טַרְזָן עַל הָעֵצִים
וְהִנֵּה הַמּוֹהִיקָנִי הָאַחֲרוֹן
מִתְגּוֹלֵל וּמֻכֶּה בָּאוֹיֵב הַלָּבָן
וִילָדִים שֶׁעוֹלָמָם דֶּלֶת אֲטוּמָה
חִדְּדוּ יְכֹלֶת הַמִּשּׁוּשׁ
לַעֲבֹר בַּחֲשָׁאִין עַל גַּבְשׁוּשִׁיּוֹת בִּנְיָר גַּס
לְגַלּוֹת אֲרָצוֹת רְחוֹקוֹת.
כָּךְ נָגְעוּ בְּתָוֵי הַפָּנִים שֶׁל הָעוֹלָם
פִּעְנְחוּ צְפָנִים הַסְּגוּרִים בְּאוֹתִיּוֹת סְתוּמוֹת
לְקַיִץ וְעוֹד קַיִץ בְּיַבָּשׁוֹת עֲלוּמוֹת

כִּי מַה לְּאִשָּׁה מְכֻבֶּדֶת כָּל כָּךְ
מִשְּׁכוּנַת רְחַבְיָה בִּירוּשָׁלַיִם
לְיֶלֶד עִוֵּר מִבֵּית חִנּוּךְ עִוְּרִים
מִתְדַּפֵּק עַל דֶּלֶת הָעוֹלָם
שֶׁקָּמָה יוֹם אֶחָד וְהֵמִירָה
קְלִידִים מְעֻדָּנִים שֶׁל פְּסַנְתֵּר
לַהֲפֹךְ אֶת יָדֶיהָ לְאֶצְבָּעוֹת מְסֻקָּסוֹת
לְהַכּוֹת בְּנִקִישׁוֹת קָשׁוֹת עַל מְכוֹנַת הַבַּרְזֶל
לְהַעֲנִיק מַפְתֵּחַ וְעוֹד מַפְתֵּחַ לְשַׁעַר הָעוֹלָם

Some of the kids
went on to universities
tracking books of reasoning and knowledge
books by Spinoza and Hegel

We always remembered you
your diligence, days and nights,
your graceful fingers turning callused
having replaced children's piano keys
with the hard keys of a Braille machine.

וְיֵשׁ מֵהֶם
שֶׁצָּלְחוּ אוּנִיבֶרְסִיטָאוֹת
בְּסִפְרֵי הָגוּת וְיֶדַע
בְּשְׁפִּינוֹזָה וּבְהֵיגֶל

זָכַרְנוּ לָךְ
אֶת שְׁקִידָתֵךְ בַּיָּמִים וּשְׁקִידָתֵךְ בַּלֵּילוֹת
שֶׁל אֶצְבָּעוֹת מְעֻדָּנוֹת שֶׁנַּעֲשׂוּ מְסֻקָּסוֹת
שֶׁהֵמִירוּ קְלִידֵי פְּסַנְתֵּר שֶׁל יְלָדִים
לְנִקִּישׁוֹת נֻקְשׁוֹת עַל מְכוֹנַת הַבְּרַיִל.

On Top of a Wall

The remains of the house fall on top of a wall
and I stand to draw living spaces
to post signs for the breaths of night, the tumults of day,
my entire being now attentive, alert,
and all that is left in me of a life's work,
of small joys laced with great pain,
is the smoky echo of remembrance

I stand at the edge of the void and say:
Here my mother held ailing brothers during the night
and here my father stood wearing his *tefilin* facing the Wailing Wall
always facing the Wailing Wall

And I draft corrections in the empty lot:
Here's a correction for the ruins of the kitchen
and here's a correction for the ruins of the bath
to cover the pudency of ashes
with tiles of innocence
hoping to redress shame

And now when all that remains of the house is a void
I stand and conjure for myself a past and a place
that had turned to dust

עַל גַּב קִיר

עַל גַּב קִיר נוֹפֵל שְׁאֵרִית הַבַּיִת
אֲנִי עוֹמֵד לְסַרְטֵט מְקוֹמוֹת חַיִּים
לְהַעֲמִיד סִימָנִים לִנְשִׁימוֹת לַיְלָה, לְמְהוּמוֹת יוֹם
עַכְשָׁו קַשׁוּב עַד הַקָּצֶה, דָּרוּךְ מִבִּפְנִים
שֶׁכָּל מַה שֶּׁנּוֹתַר בִּי מִמְּלֶאכֶת חַיִּים שְׁלֵמָה
שְׂמָחוֹת קְטַנּוֹת שְׁזוּרוֹת בִּכְאֵבִים גְּדוֹלִים
רַק הֵד עָשָׁן שֶׁל זִכָּרוֹן

אֲנִי עוֹמֵד עַל דֹּפֶן הָרִיק וְאוֹמֵר:
כָּאן הָיְתָה מַחְזִיקָה אִמִּי אַחִים חוֹלִים בַּלַּיְלָה
וְכָאן הָיָה עוֹמֵד אָבִי עִם תְּפִלִּין אֶל מוּל הַכֹּתֶל,
תָּמִיד אֶל מוּל הַכֹּתֶל

וַאֲנִי רוֹשֵׁם תִּקּוּנִים בְּשֶׁטַח רֵיק:
הִנֵּה תִּקּוּן לַהֲרִיסוֹת הַמִּטְבָּח
וְהִנֵּה תִּקּוּן לַהֲרִיסוֹת הָרַחְצָה
וּלְכַסּוֹת אֶת בֹּשֶׁת הֶעָפָר
בְּמַרְצָפוֹת שֶׁל תְּמִימוּת
שֶׁל תִּקְוָה לַהֲסָרַת בּוּשָׁה

וְעַכְשָׁו, שֶׁמִּן הַבַּיִת נוֹתַר רַק חָלָל
אֲנִי עוֹמֵד וּמְדַמֶּה לִי עָבָר וּמְדַמֶּה לִי מָקוֹם
שֶׁנַּעֲשָׂה עָפָר

from *Timbisert, A Moroccan Bird—* *New and Selected Poems* (2009)

*

He walks past quietly.
They say, He must be writing a poem.
They do not say,
Maybe he is bleeding inside.

*

הוּא הוֹלֵךְ בְּשֶׁקֶט
אוֹמְרִים
הוּא בְּוַדַּאי מְחַבֵּר שִׁיר
הֵם לֹא אוֹמְרִים
אוּלַי דָּמָיו שׁוֹתְתִים
בִּפְנִים

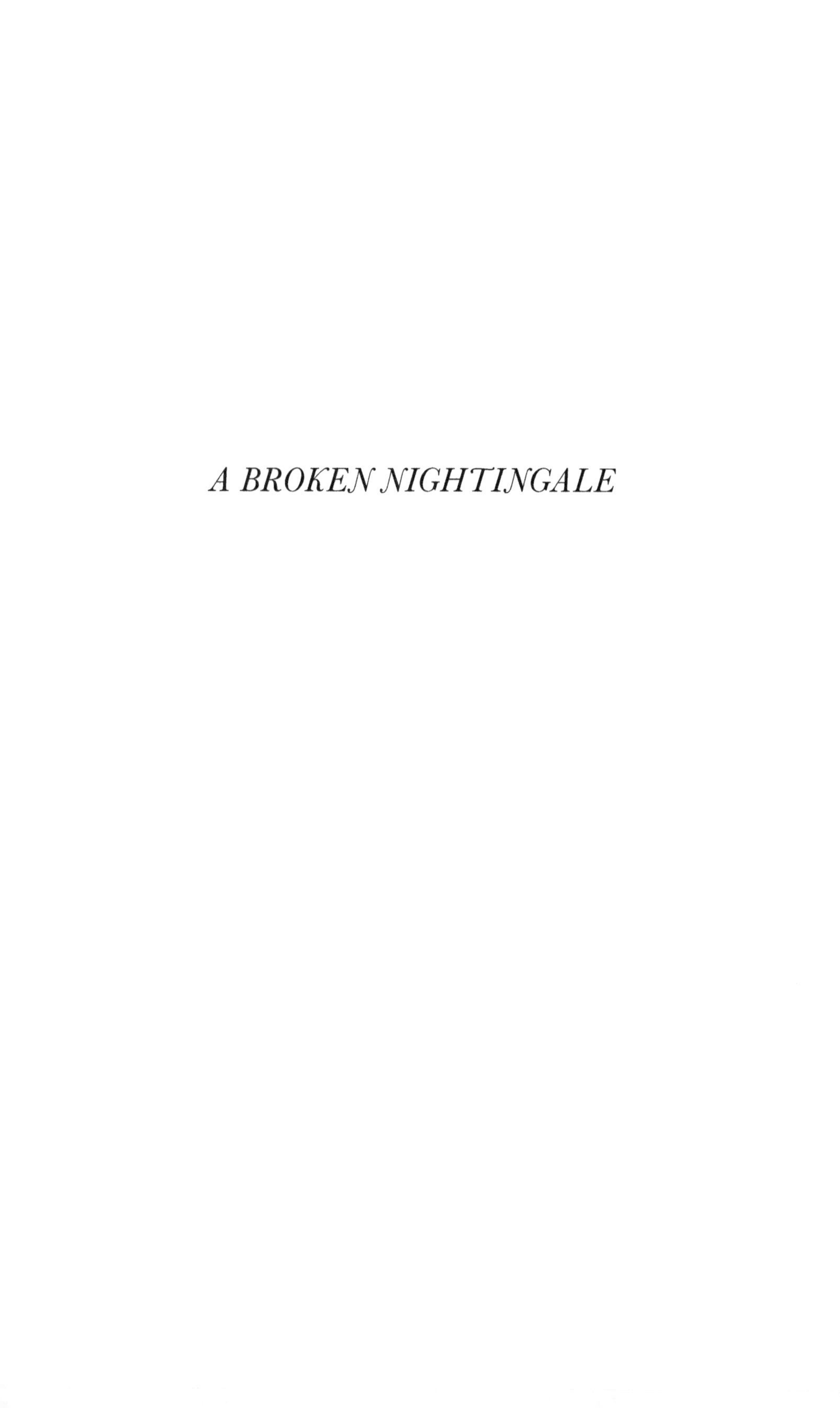

A BROKEN NIGHTINGALE

A Broken Nightingale

And in the morning the doctor said:
From now on, sir,
you remain with just one-fourth heart.
And I say:
Now where will I find
the strength for speech,
how will I walk the earth
with a broken nightingale

זמיר שבור

וְהָרוֹפֵא בַּבֹּקֶר אָמַר,
מֵעַכְשָׁו אֲדוֹנִי
אַתָּה רַק עִם רֶבַע לֵב.
וַאֲנִי אוֹמֵר,
מֵאֵיפֹה אֶמְצָא עַכְשָׁו
כּוֹחַ לְדִבּוּר,
אֵיךְ אֶסְתּוֹבֵב בָּעוֹלָם
עִם זָמִיר שָׁבוּר

Heart Valve

Why do you persist
heart valve
in growing narrower and narrower
after all you will not
filter out the sorrow in the world
you will not abate
the pain

מסתם הלב

לָמָּה אַתָּה מִתְעַקֵּשׁ
מַסְתֵּם הַלֵּב
לִהְיוֹת צַר יוֹתֵר וְיוֹתֵר
הֲרֵי לֹא תְּסַנֵּן אֶת צַעַר הָעוֹלָם
לֹא תְּמַתֵּן אֶת הַכְּאֵב

My Mother, Her Children Wouldn't Live

My mother
her children wouldn't live for her,
my mother.

The first
he wouldn't live for her,
he was named David
after her father.

The second
he wouldn't live for her,
he was named Meir
after Rabbi Meir Baal HaNess[13]
but he didn't possess the miracle of living.

The third
the third did live for her,
he was named Yaish,
which means Life
and it was me
and I lived for her.

But
some life have I lived for you,
Mother.

---

[13]See footnote 5.

לאמי, לא חיו לה הילדים

לְאִמִּי,
לֹא חָיוּ לָהּ הַיְלָדִים,
לְאִמִּי.

הָרִאשׁוֹן
לֹא חַי לָהּ הָרִאשׁוֹן,
שֶׁקָּרְאוּ לוֹ דָּוִד
עַל שֵׁם אָבִיהָ.

הַשֵּׁנִי
לֹא חַי לָהּ הַשֵּׁנִי,
שֶׁקָּרְאוּ לוֹ מֵאִיר עַל שֵׁם רַבִּי מֵאִיר בַּעַל הַנֵּס,
וְלֹא הָיָה לוֹ נֵס לִחְיוֹת.

הַשְּׁלִישִׁי
חַי לָהּ הַשְּׁלִישִׁי
שֶׁקָּרְאוּ לוֹ יְעִישׁ,
שֶׁזֶּה חַיִּים
וְזֶה הָיִיתִי אֲנִי,
וְחָיִיתִי לָהּ.

אֲבָל
אֵיזֶה חַיִּים חָיִיתִי לָהּ,
אִמִּי.

Lod Cemetery

Here lies the drunkard Slilam
whose one son makes money in Paris
whose other son in a wheelchair
begs knocking on doors
and whose daughter Juliette, killed by an Arab
who had forced her into prostitution,
ended up in a trashcan in Jaffa.

Here is Mister Massoud
upon whom in the early fifties
fortune smiled
he would stand on his truck
and deliver triumphant speeches
from the heights of the heap of trash.
He was tall and fat,
rising above us as if atop an ivory tower,
while his deaf daughter Sterra
rolled with us in beds
in a game of pillow fights
and she too
did not know she would die so young.

And here is Kmera the love of my heart
who died prematurely
and whose voice imbued us
with boundless sweetness
beyond the yard,
beyond the fence of the house,
and we did not know where to hide from her voice
that made us quiver.
During pillow fights
after she had died
her voice still hovered
across the yards.

בית הקברות בלוד

הִנֵּה כָּאן הַשִּׁכּוֹר סְלִילֶם
שֶׁבְּנוֹ הָאֶחָד עוֹשֶׂה כֶּסֶף בְּפָּרִיס
וּבְנוֹ הָאַחֵר עַל כִּסֵּא גַּלְגַּלִּים
מִתְדַּפֵּק עַל דְּלָתוֹת
וּבִתּוֹ ג'וּלְיֵט שֶׁנִּרְצְחָה בִּידֵי עַרְבִי
שֶׁהוֹרִיד אוֹתָהּ קֹדֶם לִזְנוּת
וְנִמְצְאָה לְבַסּוֹף בְּתוֹךְ פַּח אַשְׁפָּה בְּיָפוֹ.

הִנֵּה אָדוֹן מַסְעוּד
שֶׁבִּשְׁנוֹת הַחֲמִשִּׁים הַמֻּקְדָּמוֹת
שָׁפַר עָלָיו גּוֹרָלוֹ
שֶׁהָיָה עוֹמֵד עַל גַּב מַשָּׂאִית
וּמִמְּרוֹמֵי עֲרֵמוֹת הַזֶּבֶל
נוֹשֵׂא נְאוּמֵי נִצָּחוֹן
גָּבוֹהַּ וְשָׁמֵן
כְּמוֹ מֵעַל מִגְדַּל שֵׁן,
שֶׁבִּתּוֹ סְתֵרָה הַחֵרֶשֶׁת
הָיְתָה מִתְגַּלְגֶּלֶת אִתָּנוּ בַּמִּטּוֹת
בְּמִשְׂחָק שֶׁל כָּרִיּוֹת
וְגַם הִיא
לֹא יָדְעָה שֶׁתָּמוּת מֻקְדָּם כָּל כָּךְ.

הִנֵּה קָמְרָה אֲהוּבַת לִבִּי
שֶׁמֵּתָה בְּלֹא עֵת
שֶׁקּוֹלָהּ נָסַךְ עָלֵינוּ
מְתִיקוּת אֵין קֵץ
מֵעֵבֶר לֶחָצֵר
מֵעֵבֶר לְגֶדֶר הַבַּיִת
וְלֹא יָדַעְנוּ הֵיכָן לְהֵחָבֵא מִקּוֹלָהּ
שֶׁהָיָה מַכֶּה בָּנוּ רְטָטִים רְטָטִים.
מִתְגּוֹשְׁשִׁים בְּכָרִיּוֹת
לְאַחַר שֶׁמֵּתָה
נִשְׁאַר קוֹלָהּ תָּלוּי וְעוֹמֵד
מֵעַל לַחֲצֵרוֹת.

Here is Rabbi Haim and his wife
who could not stand one another while alive
it was rumored at one time
that he had splashed her with scalding water
since she was seen bandaged
from head to toe
while others softened the tale
saying she had fallen into
the Thursday wash-tub.

And here lies the old Rabbi Yitzhak
and Yisha, his blind spouse,
and I would come with him to this very cemetery
to pick dates and carobs
I would be up in the tree
tossing the fruit into the small basket
he held in his hand
and at sunset, as we walked back
with the basket laden with fruit
and I, thoroughly grateful for a day of pure joy,
would get a date or two he would generously allot me
while the golden basket
went to his blind spouse.

And here shoulder to shoulder
is our good neighbor Aharon HaCohen
nicknamed Lekvidi the Fornicator
who became a wagon peddler
having been denied a job at the airport[14]
because he would not work on the Sabbath.
We stole hay and straw for him
and Friday afternoons
we would soap his back
as he sat in the tub

---

[14]Ben Gurion Airport (formerly Lod Airport).

הִנֵּה רַבִּי חַיִּים וְאִשְׁתּוֹ
שֶׁלֹּא סָבְלוּ זֶה אֶת זוֹ בְּחַיֵּיהֶם
שֶׁפַּעַם אָמְרוּ עָלָיו
שֶׁשָּׁפַךְ עָלֶיהָ מַיִם רוֹתְחִים
כִּי נִרְאֲתָה חֲבוּשָׁה
מִכַּף רֶגֶל וְעַד רֹאשׁ
רִכְּכוּ וְאָמְרוּ
שֶׁנָּפְלָה לְגִיגִית רַחְצָה שֶׁל יוֹם חֲמִישִׁי.

וְהִנֵּה כָּאן רַבִּי יִצְחָק הַזָּקֵן
וְאִשְׁתּוֹ עִישָׁה הָעִוֶּרֶת
אִתּוֹ הָיִיתִי בָּא לְבֵית הַקְּבָרוֹת הַזֶּה מַמָּשׁ
לִקְטֹף תְּאֵנִים וְחָרוּבִים
וַאֲנִי עוֹמֵד עַל הָעֵץ
וְזוֹרֵק אֶל תּוֹךְ טֶנֶא קָטָן שֶׁבְּיָדוֹ
וּלְעֵת שְׁקִיעָה כְּשֶׁהָיִינוּ חוֹזְרִיםעִם סַל מָלֵא
הָיָה נוֹתֵן לִי בִּנְדִיבוּת לִבּוֹ
שְׁתַּיִם שָׁלוֹשׁ תְּאֵנִים
וַאֲנִי מָלֵא שִׂמְחָה מִיּוֹם שֶׁל הֲנָאָה צְרוּפָה.
אֶת הַסַּל הַזָּהֹב
הָיָה נוֹתֵן לְאִשְׁתּוֹ הָעִוֶּרֶת.

וְהִנֵּה כָּאן כָּתֵף אֶל כָּתֵף
שְׁכֵנֵנוּ הַטּוֹב אַהֲרֹן הַכֹּהֵן
הַמְּכֻנֶּה לֶקְוִידִי זַנַּאי
שֶׁנַּעֲשָׂה עֶגְלוֹן
שֶׁלֹּא קִבְּלוּ אוֹתוֹ לִשְׂדֵה הַתְּעוּפָה
כִּי שָׁמַר שַׁבָּת.
עֲבוּרוֹ הָיִינוּ גּוֹנְבִים חָצִיר וְתֶבֶן
בִּימֵי שִׁשִּׁי אַחַר הַצָּהֳרַיִם
הָיִינוּ מְסַבְּנִים אֶת גַּבּוֹ
וְהוּא יוֹשֵׁב בְּתוֹךְ גִּיגִית

white-skinned and proud of it
and whose one daughter Freha
went mad on her wedding night
and his other daughter Macha
as pretty as the moon
was nicknamed cow-eyes
einin elbegra
because you could drown in them.

And here is Avraham nicknamed Heno
they made an exception for him and did not
bury him outside the cemetery gates
even though he had committed suicide
shooting himself.
Heno
darker than dark
towering above us
as we walked between his legs
and he high and mighty
and talking to no one.

They said he was the first
to get a job at the airport
and they also said
that he had opened a café
where in the evening
he would fool around
with an Ashkenazi woman.
He buried with him
the mystery of his sudden demise
and yet also managed
to build a banquet hall
and name it after himself.

And here is the teacher of the long sidelocks
for whom we would pick flowers in this cemetery
and bring to him as an offering

לַבְנוּנִי גֵּאֶה בְּלַבְנוּנִיּוּתוֹ,
שֶׁבִּתּוֹ הָאַחַת פִּרְחָה
הִשְׁתַּגְּעָה בְּלֵיל כְּלוּלוֹתֶיהָ
וּבִתּוֹ הָאַחֶרֶת מָחָה
יָפָה כַּיָּרֵחַ
שֶׁנִּקְרְאָה עֵינֵי הַפָּרָה עֵינְיָן אֶלְבְּגְרָה
עַל שׁוּם עֵינֶיהָ שֶׁיָּכֹלְתָּ לִטְבֹּעַ בָּהֶן.

וְכָאן אַבְרָהָם הַמְכֻנֶּה הְנוֹ
וְעָשׂוּ אִתּוֹ חֶסֶד
שֶׁלֹּא טָמְנוּ אוֹתוֹ מִחוּץ לַגָּדֵר
שֶׁהֲרֵי
הִתְאַבֵּד בִּירִיָּה.
הְנוֹ
הַשָּׁחֹר מִשְּׁחוֹר
שֶׁגָּבְהוֹ מֵעַל כֻּלָּנוּ
שֶׁהָיִינוּ מְהַלְּכִים בֵּין רַגְלָיו
וְהוּא בֵּינֵינוּ רָם וְנִשָּׂא
וְלֹא מְדַבֵּר עִם אִישׁ.

עָלָיו אָמְרוּ
שֶׁהָיָה רִאשׁוֹן
שֶׁקִּבֵּל עֲבוֹדָה בִּשְׂדֵה הַתְּעוּפָה
וְגַם אָמְרוּ עָלָיו
שֶׁהֵקִים בֵּית קָפֶה לִשְׁעוֹת הָעֶרֶב
לְהִשְׁתַּעֲשֵׁעַ
עִם אִשָּׁה אַשְׁכְּנַזִּיָּה.
קָבַר אִתּוֹ אֶת חִידַת מוֹתוֹ הַפִּתְאוֹמִי
וְעוֹד הִסְפִּיק לְהָקִים אוּלַם שְׂמָחוֹת
וְלִקְרֹא אֶת שְׁמוֹ עָלָיו.

הִנֵּה הַמּוֹרֶה אֶרֶךְ הַפֵּאוֹת
שֶׁהָיִינוּ קוֹטְפִים לְמַעֲנוֹ פְּרָחִים
בְּבֵית הַקְּבָרוֹת הַזֶּה

to appease him for being late to school
but he would not relent
he took the flowers and did strike us
with the small ruler he kept in his pocket.

And here is Aharon ben Chmou
who fell in the Six-Day War.
We used to pray with him
in the small synagogue
named Mother Rachel,[15]
and he, Aharon,
during the Rosh Hashanah service,
would weep, reciting the story
of Akedat Yitzhak[16]
not knowing
he was reciting his own Akeda.

And here is the cracked gravestone of my parents
every year we plan to restore it
and don't
and now a rain is falling
seeping
and my mother who could not stand the cold
wearing a sweater
all year long.

And I, where will I be buried,
I would like to be buried here
among those who lived
in the fifties
in the town of Lod.

---

[15]A woman named Rachel who donated the funds to build the synagogue. (Author's note.)

[16]The Binding (Sacrifice) of Yitzhak (Genesis 22:5).

וּמְבִיאִים לוֹ מִנְחָה
כְּדֵי לְרַצּוֹת אוֹתוֹ מִפְּנֵי אֲחוֹרֵנוּ
אֲבָל הוּא לֹא הִתְעַשֵּׁת
גַּם לָקַח וְגַם הִכָּה
בְּסַרְגֵּל קָטָן שֶׁהָיָה בְּכִיסוֹ.

וְהִנֵּה הָרוֹן בֶּן חָמוּ
שֶׁנָּפַל בְּמִלְחֶמֶת שֵׁשֶׁת הַיָּמִים
אִתּוֹ הָיִינוּ מִתְפַּלְּלִים
בְּבֵית הַכְּנֶסֶת הַקָּטָן
עַל שֵׁם אִמָּא רָחֵל.
וְהוּא הָרוֹן,
הָיָה עוֹמֵד בְּרֹאשׁ הַשָּׁנָה
וְקוֹרֵא בְּבֶכִי אֶת עֲקֵדַת יִצְחָק
וְלֹא יָדַע
שֶׁקָּרָא אֶת הָעֲקֵדָה שֶׁל עַצְמוֹ.

וְהִנֵּה כָּאן קֶבֶר הוֹרַי הַסָּדוּק
שֶׁאֲנַחְנוּ אוֹמְרִים כָּל שָׁנָה לְתַקֵּן
וְלֹא מְתַקְּנִים
וְגֶשֶׁם יוֹרֵד עַכְשָׁו
וּמְחַלְחֵל
וְאִמִּי שֶׁלֹּא עָמְדָה בִּפְנֵי הַקֹּר
שֶׁלֹּא פָּשְׁטָה מֵעָלֶיהָ
אֶת הַסְּוֶדֶר כָּל הַשָּׁנָה.

וַאֲנִי הֵיכָן אֶטָּמֵן
הָיִיתִי רוֹצָה לְהִטָּמֵן כָּאן
בֵּין הַחַיִּים
בִּשְׁנוֹת הַחֲמִשִּׁים
בָּעִיר לֹד.

At Sunset

At sunset
in the Land of Israel
my father would expose
his arm and say:
From the elbow up
all that's clear and clean
from the elbow down
down to the fingertips
all that's darkened
scorched
damaged
spent.
And I say to him:
Your heart may be up in the sky
but your face looks to the ground
and you, Father,
are a father
scarred.

בשעה של שקיעה

בְּשָׁעָה שֶׁל שְׁקִיעָה
בְּאֶרֶץ יִשְׂרָאֵל
אָבִי הָיָה חוֹשֵׂף
אֶת זְרוֹעוֹ וְאוֹמֵר:
מִן הַמַּרְפֵּק וּלְמַעְלָה
כָּל הַבָּהִיר וְהַמְנֻקֶּה
וּמִן הַמַּרְפֵּק וּלְמַטָּה
וְעַד לְשֹׁרֶשׁ הָאֶצְבָּעוֹת
כָּל הַמֻּכְהֶה
וְהַצָּרוּב
וְהַלָּקוּי
וְהַנִּפְקָע.
וַאֲנִי אוֹמֵר לוֹ:
לִבְּךָ אוּלַי בַּשָּׁמַיִם
אֲבָל פָּנֶיךָ בַּקַּרְקַע
וְאַתָּה אַבָּא
אַתָּה אַבָּא
מְקֻעְקָע.

On Winter Mornings

On winter mornings
my mother would make
Hrira soup[17]
mixing in her warmth on a cold day
spicing it with the grace of her heart

Against broken blinds
three or four of us in one bed
sitting around the steaming pot
our lost yearnings rising in the mist

It is there, Mother,
that I divined for you
a bit of warmth in cold days
it is there that I wove for you
oaths
of summers to come

---

[17] A Jewish-Moroccan vegetable soup.

בבקרים של חורף

בִּבְקָרִים שֶׁל חֹרֶף
עָשְׂתָה אִמִּי מָרָק שֶׁל חֲרִירָה
מָסְכָה בּוֹ מִמֶּנָּה חֹם בְּיוֹם קַר
וְתִבְּלָה אוֹתוֹ בְּחֶמְדַּת לִבָּהּ.

אֶל מוּל תְּרִיסִים שְׁבוּרִים
שְׁלוֹשָׁה וְאַרְבָּעָה בְּמִטָּה אַחַת
סָבִיב לְסִיר מַעֲלֶה אֵדִים
שָׁם עָלוּ כְּמִיהוֹתֵינוּ הָאֲבוּדוֹת.

שָׁם הֲכַנְתִּי לָךְ אִמִּי
מְעַט חֹם לְיָמִים קָרִים
שָׁם רָקַמְתִּי לָךְ אִמִּי
הַבְטָחוֹת
לְקַיִץ רַב.

For Aharon ben Chmou

And still Aharon ben Chmou
reciting his own Akeda
year after year
in the small synagogue of Mother Rachel
in the town of Lod
Aharon ben Chmou
reciting out loud his own Sacrifice
with the excitation of facing the congregation,
and they try to cue him
to let others
read Akedat Yitzhak
during the Days of Awe,
but he, again and again,
insists on reciting
his own Akeda.

Aharon ben Chmou
who fell in the Six-Day War.

לאהרון בן חמו

וְעוֹד אַהֲרֹן בֶּן חְמוּ
קוֹרֵא אֶת הָעֲקֵדָה שֶׁל עַצְמוֹ
מִדֵּי שָׁנָה בְּשָׁנָה
בְּבֵית הַכְּנֶסֶת הַקָּטָן שֶׁל אִמָּא רָחֵל
בָּעִיר לוּד
אַהֲרֹן בֶּן חְמוּ
קוֹרֵא אֶת הָעֲקֵדָה שֶׁל עַצְמוֹ
בְּהִתְרַגְּשׁוּת שֶׁל עֲמִידָה בְּקָהָל,
וּמְבַקְשִׁים לִרְמֹז לוֹ
לְהַנִּיחַ לַאֲחֵרִים
לִקְרֹא אֶת עֲקֵדַת יִצְחָק
בַּיָּמִים הַנּוֹרָאִים.
אֲבָל
הוּא מִתְעַקֵּשׁ שׁוּב וָשׁוּב
לִקְרֹא אֶת הָעֲקֵדָה שֶׁל עַצְמוֹ.

אַהֲרֹן בֶּן חְמוּ
שֶׁנָּפַל בְּמִלְחֶמֶת שֵׁשֶׁת הַיָּמִים.

Ballad About a Town at Sunset

The sun set beyond the cactus hedge.
An Arab woman wearing a headscarf
bends down to collect stubbles in the field
it is the season
the soft rays of the sun
have transformed
right before our eyes
a bundle of hay
into a human figure
both friendly and ominous
evoking our mothers
and now
as the sun has sunk
a rush of anxiety to go back
breaks open in us
a worry for the one
who worries about us at home
the mother who at this very moment
is surely knocking on neighbors' doors
asking where is he
have you seen him
was one of your kids with him
and presently she walks in the streets
calling:
"Zaish, Zaish"
and only the echo answers her
and then in all probability
at some intersection
she will meet by chance
the mother of my friend Gabi
who's walking beside me
and she too is calling in vain:
"Gabi, Gabi"
and our two mothers will vow

בלדה על עיר בשקיעה

הַשְּׁקִיעָה הָיְתָה מֵעֵבֶר לְגֶדֶר הַסַּבְּרֶס.
אִשָּׁה עַרְבִיָּה עִם מִטְפַּחַת רֹאשׁ
רְכוּנָה לְלַקֵּט בַּשָּׂדֶה בְּעוֹנַת הַשֶּׁלֶף
קַרְנֵי הַשֶּׁמֶשׁ הָרַכּוֹת
הָפְכוּ לְעֵינֵינוּ
חֲבִילָה שֶׁל חָצִיר
לִדְמוּת אֱנוֹשִׁית מַרְתִּיעָה וִידִידוּתִית גַּם יַחַד
הַמַּזְכִּירָה אֶת אִמּוֹתֵינוּ
עַכְשָׁו
שֶׁקָּרְסָה הַשֶּׁמֶשׁ לְגַמְרֵי
נִפְתַּח בָּנוּ
רֶגֶשׁ בָּהוּל לְהֵחָפֵז מִפְּנֵי הַדְּאָגָה
לַזֹּאת הַדּוֹאֶגֶת לָנוּ בַּבַּיִת
הָאִמָּא שֶׁבְּרֶגַע זֶה בְּוַדַּאי מִתְדַּפֶּקֶת עַל פִּתְחֵי הַשְּׁכֵנִים
וְשׁוֹאֶלֶת אֵיפֹה הוּא
הַאִם מִישֶׁהוּ רָאָה
הַאִם אַחַד הַיְלָדִים שֶׁלָּכֶם הָיָה אִתּוֹ,
וְאַחַר כָּךְ הִיא מְהַלֶּכֶת בָּרְחוֹבוֹת
וְקוֹרֵאת
"זַיְשׁ זַיְשׁ"
רַק הַהֵד עוֹנֶה לָהּ
וְאָז קָרוֹב לְוַדַּאי
תִּפְגֹּשׁ בְּאַקְרַאי
בְּצֹמֶת הַסִּמְטָאוֹת
אֶת אִמּוֹ שֶׁל חֲבֵרִי גַּבִּי
הַהוֹלֵךְ כָּאן לְצִדִּי
וְגַם הִיא
קוֹרֵאת לַשָּׁוְא
"גַּבִּי גַּבִּי"
וּשְׁתֵּי אִמּוֹתֵנוּ יִדְּרוּ נֶדֶר וְיִשָּׁבְעוּ בְּאֶלֶף שְׁבוּעוֹת

and pledge a thousand pledges
that tomorrow they will ground us
and this realization of our mothers' anguish
at this very moment
rouses sadness in us
and longing and anger as well
as if some force has cut short
the flow of an everlasting day
arbitrarily setting a limit for us
and a gaping longing spreads in us
for the mother we haven't seen all day
and who nevertheless has dwelled the entire time
at the edge of our consciousness
we must go back home.
From here
from beyond the railway tracks
from the orchards of Lod
rise the sound of crickets
which amplifies as if with a megaphone
the feeling of sadness
the immeasurable longing
accelerating our walk into a harried run
and only now
we feel a sudden pressing hunger
we haven't felt all day,
and after the scolding that awaits us at home
possibly even a smack of anger and anguish
across the back or on the arm,
after we stand at a safe distance from the house
negotiating with the mothers not to punish us,
only then will we slip inside
directly into the kitchen
where no doubt a pot
of skinny noodles spiced with pepper
is ready
or, if we're lucky,
we'll find on the table

שֶׁיִּסְגְּרוּ אוֹתָנוּ לַמָּחֳרָת בַּבַּיִת
הַיְדִיעָה הַזֹּאת שֶׁל דַּאֲגַת הָאֵם
בְּעֶצֶם הָרֶגַע הַזֶּה
מְעוֹרֶרֶת בָּנוּ עִצָּבוֹן
גַּעֲגוּעִים וְכַעַס גַּם יַחַד,
כְּאִלּוּ מַשֶּׁהוּ קוֹטֵעַ אֶת רֶצֶף הַיּוֹם שֶׁאֵין לוֹ גְּבוּל
וְהִנֵּה בִּשְׁרִירוּת לֵב
תּוֹחֲמִים לָנוּ גְּבוּל
וְנִפְעָר בָּנוּ גַּעֲגוּעַ לָאֵם
שֶׁכָּל הַיּוֹם לֹא רְאִינוּ
וְלַמְרוֹת זֹאת שָׁכְנָה כָּל הָעֵת בְּשׁוּלֵי הַתּוֹדָעָה שֶׁלָּנוּ
אֲנַחְנוּ חַיָּבִים לַחְזֹר הַבַּיְתָה
מִכָּאן
מֵעֵבֶר לְמְסִלַּת הַבַּרְזֶל
מִן הַפַּרְדֵּסִים שֶׁל לֹד
קוֹלוֹת הַצְּרָצָרִים מַגְבִּירִים כְּמוֹ בְּרַמְקוֹל
אֶת תְּחוּשַׁת הָעִצָּבוֹן
וְאֶת הַגַּעֲגוּעִים הָאֵין סוֹפִיִּים
שֶׁהָפְכוּ אֶת הֲלִיכָתֵנוּ לְרִיצָה מְבֹהֶלֶת.
רַק עַכְשָׁו
אֲנַחְנוּ מַרְגִּישִׁים פִּתְאוֹם רָעָב דָּחוּף
מַה שֶּׁלֹּא הִרְגַּשְׁנוּ כָּל הַיּוֹם
לְאַחַר הַנְּזִיפָה הַמְזֻמֶּנֶת לָנוּ בְּפֶתַח הַבַּיִת
אוּלַי גַּם מַכָּה שֶׁל כַּעַס וְצַעַר עַל הַגַּב אוֹ הַזְּרוֹעַ
לְיֶתֶר בִּטָּחוֹן נַעֲמֹד בְּמֶרְחָק מֵהַבַּיִת
לָשֵׂאת וְלָתֵת עִם הָאֵם
שֶׁלֹּא תִּגַּע בָּנוּ לְרָעָה
וְרַק אָז נֶחְמַק פְּנִימָה
יָשָׁר לַמִּטְבָּח שָׁם
נָכוֹן לָנוּ בְּוַדַּאי
סִיר שֶׁל אִטְרִיּוֹת דַּקּוֹת
מְטֻבָּלוֹת בְּפִלְפֵּל חָרִיף
אוֹ יָאִיר לָנוּ הַמַּזָּל יוֹתֵר
וְנִמְצָא עַל הַשֻּׁלְחָן בַּמִּטְבָּח

a bowl of roasted peppers and tomatoes
what we call Salata Matbucha
and then we'll climb onto the bed
with the two small brothers long asleep
and we too will fall asleep at once
without further ado

קַעֲרַת סָלָט מְבֻשָּׁל
הַקָּרוּי אֶצְלֵנוּ סָלָטָה מַטְבּוּחָה
וְאָז נִכָּנֵס לַמִּטָּה
עִם שְׁנֵי הָאַחִים הַקְּטַנִּים אֲשֶׁר נִרְדְּמוּ מִכְּבָר
וְנֵרָדֵם גַּם אֲנַחְנוּ מִיָּד
לְלֹא הִרְהוּרִים נוֹסָפִים

The Wail of Women

Ten women on the roofs
spreading their arms
to cry the cry of their dead sons

Ten women
gathered from the nooks and alleyways
having abandoned their pots and lids
the damp wash hanging in the *patio*[18]
and infants laughing in their cribs

Ten women
hello ten women
collect all the nard
collect all the roses
bathing the *patio* with their fragrance
collect all the candles
to light a memorial candle

Ten women
ten women on the roofs
their arms spread

Hello Aunt Esther
how are you tonight
hello Aunt Fortuna
how are you doing
and you, Saida,
and you, Klara,
and you who have yet to go up to the roof
bring forth your sons

---

[18]Inner courtyard.

בכי הנשים

עֶשֶׂר נָשִׁים עַל הַגַּגּוֹת
פְּרוּשׂוֹת יָדַיִם
לִצְעֹק אֶת צַעֲקַת בְּנָן הַמֵּת.

עֶשֶׂר נָשִׁים
הִתְקַבְּצוּ מִן הַכּוּכִים וְהַסִּמְטָאוֹת
אֶת סִירֵיהֶן הִשְׁלִיכוּ בְּמִכְסִים זְרוּקִים
וְהַכְּבִיסָה תְּלוּיָה בְּפַצְעוֹ וְהָאָרִיג לַח
וְתִינוֹקוֹת צוֹחֲקִים בַּעֲרִיסוֹת.

עֶשֶׂר נָשִׁים
הֵי עֶשֶׂר נָשִׁים
אִסְפוּ אֶת כָּל הַנֵּרְדְּ
וְאֶת כָּל הַשּׁוֹשָׁן
הַנּוֹתֵן רֵיחוֹ בְּפִצְעוֹ
אִסְפוּ אֶת כָּל הַנֵּרוֹת
לְהַדְלִיק נֵר שֶׁל נְשָׁמוֹת.

עֶשֶׂר נָשִׁים
עֶשֶׂר נָשִׁים עַל הַגַּגּוֹת
פְּרוּשׂוֹת יָדַיִם

הֵי דּוֹדָה אֶסְתֵּר
מַה שְּׁלוֹמֵךְ הַלַּיְלָה
הֵי דּוֹדָה פוֹרְטוּנָה.
מַה שְּׁלוֹמְכֶן
אַתְּ סָעִידָה
וְאַתְּ קְלָרָה
וְאַתֶּן שֶׁעֲדַיִן אֵינְכֶן עַל הַגַּגּוֹת
הוֹצִיאוּ אֶת בְּנֵיכֶן

to display their white teeth
their astonishing bearings
the curve of their gentle hands
the scent of roses rising from their breaths

Hello ten women
tell them that the announcement will come
before too long

Do not go back to your pots
bubbling steams of peace
do not go back to the laughter of your babies

Remain on the rooftops
and all the holy Jews
and all the holy Christians
and all the holy Muslims
will stand on the roofs
beside you
their arms spread
to cry with you
the cry of your dead sons

Hello ten women

לְהַרְאוֹת אֶת שִׁנֵּיהֶם הַלְּבָנוֹת
אֶת קוֹמָתָם שֶׁלֹּא תֵּאָמֵן
אֶת קִמּוּרֵי יְדֵיהֶם הָעֲדִינִים
אֶת רֵיחַ הַשּׁוֹשָׁן הַבָּא מִנִּשְׁימָתָם.

הֵי עֶשֶׂר נָשִׁים
אִמְרוּ לָהֶם כִּי הַיְדִיעָה בּוֹא תָּבוֹא
כִּי הַיְדִיעָה לֹא תְּאַחֵר לָבוֹא

אַל תָּשׁוּבוּ אֶל הַסִּירִים
מַעֲלֵי אֵדִים שֶׁל שָׁלוֹם
אַל תָּשׁוּבוּ לִצְחוֹק הַתִּינוֹקוֹת

כִּי עַל הַגַּגּוֹת תִּהְיֶינָה
וְכָל הַקְּדוֹשִׁים הַיְּהוּדִים
וְכָל הַנּוֹצְרִים
וְכָל הַקְּדוֹשִׁים הַמֻּסְלְמִים
יַעַמְדוּ לְצִדְּכֶן
עַל הַגַּגּוֹת
בְּיָדַיִם פְּרוּשׂוֹת
לִצְעֹק אִתְּכֶן
אֶת צַעֲקַת בִּנְכֶן הַמֵּת

הֵי עֶשֶׂר נָשִׁים

Lullaby in the Town of Oran

1.
"Elijah the Prophet"
my mother shouted.
"It's Elijah the Prophet"
my father called out—
Elijah who had appeared in his dream
to sit with him and recite
a chapter from the Book of Psalms.
And I rise and run out
of the house that is a room
that is a wall falling upon a falling wall
and my father and mother
grab the hem of my tiny garment
so I won't fly away
so I won't run away
so I won't break away
from myself
there in the town of Oran in Algeria
and I'm three or four years old
and where can I flee
and where will I fall
and where will I run from Elijah the Prophet
and I know that this evening again
my father will head the procession of the dead
wearing his finest
and I know that tonight again my father will go
to Hevra Kadisha[19] to sit with the dead
hold the hands of the dying with iron and brass
to chase away all evil till morning[20]

---

[19]Jewish burial society.

[20]A Jewish-Moroccan custom to ward off evil spirits with objects made of iron and brass.

שיר שינה בעיר אוראן

א.
"אֵלִיָּהוּ הַנָּבִיא"
צָעֲקָה אִמִּי
"זֶה אֵלִיָּהוּ הַנָּבִיא"
קָרָא אָבִי
שֶׁנִּכְנַס לוֹ לַחֲלוֹם
לָשֶׁבֶת אִתּוֹ וּלְשַׁנֵּן
פֶּרֶק מִתְּהִלִּים
וַאֲנִי קָם וְרָץ וְיוֹצֵא
מֵהַבַּיִת שֶׁהוּא חֶדֶר
שֶׁהוּא קִיר נוֹפֵל עַל קִיר נוֹפֵל
וְאִמִּי וְאָבִי תּוֹפְסִים בְּשׁוּלֵי בִּגְדִי הַקָּטָן
שֶׁלֹּא אָעוּף
שֶׁלֹּא אֶבְרַח
שֶׁלֹּא אֵצֵא
מִתּוֹךְ עַצְמִי לְגַמְרֵי
שָׁם בָּעִיר אוֹרָן שֶׁבְּאַלְגִּ'יר
וַאֲנִי בֶּן שָׁלוֹשׁ אוֹ אַרְבַּע
וַאֲנִי לְאָן אֶבְרַח
וּלְאָן אֶפֹּל
וּלְאָן אֵצֵא מֵאֵלִיָּהוּ הַנָּבִיא
וַאֲנִי יוֹדֵעַ שֶׁגַּם הָעֶרֶב
יֵלֵךְ אָבִי בְּרֹאשׁ תַּהֲלוּכַת הַמֵּתִים בְּבִגְדֵי חֲמוּדוֹת
וַאֲנִי יוֹדֵעַ שֶׁגַּם הַלַּיְלָה אָבִי יֵלֵךְ לְחֶבְרָא קַדִּישָׁא
לָשֶׁבֶת לִמְרַאֲשׁוֹת הַמֵּתִים
לְהַחְזִיק בִּידֵי הַגּוֹסְסִים בְּמִינֵי בַּרְזֶל וּנְחֹשֶׁת לְהַבְרִיחַ מַזִּיקִים
עַד לַבֹּקֶר

when the dead depart together
with Elijah the Prophet

2.
Today I am with you,
child,
I will release you from a troubled sleep.
Hand in hand
no longer fearing falling
down a terrible void
together with you I will leave the room
that is a wall upon a wall
together we will ascend the street
slowly and gently sloping upward
and I will teach you
how to reach the divine chariots
I will teach you
how to be in a sleep to last till morning
together we will arrive at the cave of Elijah the Prophet
as if at a magical cave
and even with Baal and Ashtoreth[21]
we shall dwell in peace

---

[21]Pagan gods.

עַד לְצֵאתָם יַחַד
עִם אֵלִיָּהוּ הַנָּבִיא

ב.
הַיּוֹם אֲנִי אִתְּךָ
יֶלֶד
אוֹצִיא אוֹתְךָ מִתּוֹךְ שֵׁנָה מֻכָּה.
יָד בְּיָד
לֹא עוֹד בְּפַחַד שֶׁל נְפִילוֹת
אֶל חָלָל נוֹרָא
אֵצֵא עִמְּךָ מִן הַחֶדֶר
שֶׁהוּא קִיר עַל קִיר
אִתְּךָ נַעֲלֶה בְּמַעֲלֵה הָרְחוֹב
הַמְּטַפֵּס לְאַט וּבְשֶׁקֶט
אֲלַמֵּד אוֹתְךָ
לְהַגִּיעַ אֶל הַמֶּרְכָּבוֹת הַטּוֹבוֹת
אֲלַמֵּד אוֹתְךָ
לִהְיוֹת בְּתוֹךְ שֵׁנָה שֶׁל עַד הַבֹּקֶר
יַחַד אִתְּךָ נַגִּיעַ אֶל מְעָרַת אֵלִיָּהוּ הַנָּבִיא
כְּמוֹ אֶל מְעָרַת קְסָמִים
וַאֲפִלּוּ עִם הַבַּעַל וְהָעַשְׁתֹּרֶת
נִחְיֶה בְּשָׁלוֹם

We Are Strangers[22]

We are strangers
and strangeness burnt our eyes
from weeping
and if we die
Arab women going past
will say:
This man is a stranger
Let us throw over him a handful of earth
so jackals don't get to him.
And I say:
Let us recall a time of grace
so we don't throw at one another
fistfuls of dirt.

---

[22]After a Jewish-Moroccan song about Jews, expelled from Spain (1492), dying on the shores of Morocco. (Author's note.)

אנחנו זרים

אֲנַחְנוּ זָרִים
וְהַזָּרוּת כָּוְתָה את עֵינֵינוּ
מִבֶּכִי
וְאִם נָמוּת
נָשִׁים עַרְבִיּוֹת תַּעֲבֹרְנָה
תֹּאמַרְנָה
הָאִישׁ הַזֶּה זָר
נִזְרֹק עָלָיו קֹמֶץ עָפָר
שֶׁלֹּא יֹאכַל אוֹתוֹ הַתַּן.
וַאֲנִי אוֹמֵר
בּוֹאוּ נִזְכֹּר חֶסֶד עָבָר
שֶׁלֹּא נִזְרֹק אֵלֶּה עַל אֵלֶּה
חוּפְנִים שֶׁל עָפָר.

Spanish Song

Their hearts are steeped
in a solution of birdsong
and the scent of flowers
will knock against their walls
will knock till they bleed
against the heavy locks
and the many locks will reverberate
and our longings will age
within the iron chests.
And we are steeped in the warm
liquid matter from where the strain
of their love will not break through
but will only knock with tight fists
against the many locks
and only with their hearts
will they be able to share
the wailing of their drenched hearts.
The song of birds will render
the image of their beloved
in nard and turmeric
in the blessing of longevity
and will commemorate their short lives
as a page in one of their weighty books.
During moments at the seam of night and day
you've unraveled yourself down to the thread's end
disgorging your anguish in a clear saying
bare-boned in its simplicity.

שיר ספרדי

לִבָּם שָׁרוּי
בְּתְמִיסַת קוֹלוֹת הַצִּפּוֹרִים
וְרֵיחוֹת הַפְּרָחִים
יַכּוּ עַל דָּפְנוֹתֵיהֶם
מַכִּים עַד זוֹב דָּם בַּמַּנְעוּלִים הַכְּבֵדִים
וּמְאוֹת הַמַּנְעוּלִים יְהַדְהֲדוּ
וּכְמִיהוֹתֵינוּ יַזְקִינוּ
בְּתֵבוֹת הַבַּרְזֶל
וַאֲנַחְנוּ שְׁרוּיִים בַּחֹמֶר הַחַם וְהַנּוֹזֵל
מִשָּׁם לֹא תֵּצֵא תְּעוּקַת אַהֲבָתָם
רַק תַּכֶּה בְּאֶגְרוֹפִים קְמוּצִים
בִּמְאוֹת הַמַּנְעוּלִים
וְרַק עִם לִבָּם יוּכְלוּ לְחַלֵּק
אֶת נַאֲקַת לִבָּם הַשָּׁרוּי בִּתְמִיסוֹת
קוֹלוֹת הַצִּפּוֹרִים יְצַיְּרוּ אֶת דְּמוּת אֲהוּבָתָם
בְּנֵרְדְּ וְכַרְכֹּם
בִּסְגֻלּוֹת אֲרִיכוּת הַיּוֹמִין
וְיַנְצִיחוּ אֶת חַיֵּיהֶם הַקְּצָרִים
כְּדַף בְּסֵפֶר מִסִּפְרֵיהֶם הַכְּבֵדִים.
בְּרִגְעֵי הַתֶּפֶר בֵּין לַיְלָה לְיוֹם
פָּרַמְתָּ אֶת עַצְמְךָ עַד סוֹף הַחוּט
מֵקִיא אֶת סִבְלְךָ בַּאֲמִירָה נְקִיָּה
וּפְשׁוּטָה עַד הָעֶצֶם.

Clipped Orange Trees

Clipped orange trees
a lying testimony to calm,
a deep well in the *patio*
a lying testimony to calm,
ancient olives and the hum of the sea
it is all a lie
since under this veneer, this calm
there's another calm,
a calm that is fear
the fear of knocking down locks
the fear of homes
that might break open
with sagging walls.

How did the flamenco begin
in a room within a shut room,
the navel of the universe,
and the crowd outside
only a false alibi.

At first
the drumming fingers
of an old woman and a child
upon wooden tables
with the hesitancy of a hint
at a contained zest for life
barely audible at first
and only then
comes the uncontrollable dance
the frenzied stomping feet
for the dance comes
when there's nothing more to lose
when the intruders are not at the door

עצי תפוז קצוצי ענף

עֲצֵי תַּפּוּז קְצוּצֵי עָנָף
עֵדוּת שֶׁקֶר לְשֶׁקֶט,
בְּאֵר עֲמֻקָּה בְּפַאצְיוֹ
עֵדוּת שֶׁקֶר שֶׁל שֶׁקֶט,
זֵיתִים עַתִּיקִים וְרַחַשׁ יָם
הַכֹּל שֶׁקֶר
כִּי מִתַּחַת לַמַּסְוֶה, לַשֶּׁקֶט הַזֶּה
יֵשׁ שֶׁקֶט אַחֵר,
שֶׁקֶט שֶׁהוּא פַּחַד
פַּחַד הַמַּכִּים בַּמַּנְעוּלִים
פַּחַד הַבָּתִּים
הָעֲלוּלִים לִהְיוֹת פְּעוּרִים
עִם קִירוֹת נְפוּלִים.

אֵיךְ הִתְחִיל הַפְּלָמֶנְקוֹ
בְּחֶדֶר לִפְנֵי מֵחֶדֶר סָגוּר
שֶׁהוּא טַבּוּר הָעוֹלָם
וְהַקָּהָל בַּחוּץ
הוּא רַק אָלִיבִּי שָׁגוּי.

כִּי בַּהַתְחָלָה
נְקִישׁוֹת הָאֶצְבָּעוֹת
שֶׁל זְקֵנָה וְיֶלֶד
עַל שֻׁלְחָנוֹת שֶׁל עֵץ
בְּהִסּוּס שֶׁל רֶמֶז
לְשִׂמְחַת חַיִּים עֲצוּרָה
כִּמְעַט בְּלִי קוֹל
וְרַק אַחַר כָּךְ
בָּא הָרִקּוּד הַבִּלְתִּי נִשְׁלָט
בְּמַכּוֹת תְּזָזִית בָּרַגְלַיִם
כִּי הָרִקּוּד בָּא
כְּשֶׁאֵין כְּבָר מַה לְּהַפְסִיד
כְּשֶׁהַפּוֹרְצִים
אֵינָם עַל סַף הַבַּיִת

but are inside already
when the homes gape open to the sky
and the sagging walls collapse
now
a tight flamenco
for a cheap ticket in Madrid
the lust for life travels
from fingertips to soles
gnarled feet in the caves of Granada.

This is how flamenco began
an old woman and a child
a locked room and a fear
and a great desire
to shout Life.

כִּי אִם פְּנִימָה
כְּשֶׁהַבָּתִּים פְּעוּרִים לַשָּׁמַיִם
וְהַקִּירוֹת מִתְמוֹטְטִים נְפוּלִים
עַכְשָׁו
פְלָמֶנְקוֹ הָדוּק
בְּכַרְטִיסִים זוֹלִים בְּמַדְרִיד
הַתְּשׁוּקָה לַחַיִּים עוֹבֶרֶת
מִן הָאֶצְבָּעוֹת אֶל כַּפּוֹת הָרַגְלַיִם
רַגְלַיִם מְסֻקָּסוֹת בִּמְעָרוֹת גְּרָנָדָה.

כָּךְ הִתְחִיל הַפְלָמֶנְקוֹ
אִשָּׁה זְקֵנָה וְיֶלֶד
וְחֶדֶר סָגוּר וּפַחַד
וּתְשׁוּקָה גְּדוֹלָה
לִצְעֹק חַיִּים.

Poem at the Heart of Jerusalem

A man walks down the street

He doesn't know that a thousand eyes watch him

He'd better walk slowly
let them not think
he is chasing after his dreams

He always
has a poem with him
but what use is the poem contained in him

The poem mitigates his desire to devour distances

And he must know
that even if he stops walking
he will arrive

For he is always
at the heart of Jerusalem

שיר באמצע ירושלים

אִישׁ הוֹלֵךְ בָּרְחוֹב

הוּא אֵינוֹ יוֹדֵעַ שֶׁאֶלֶף עֵינַיִם מְצִיצוֹת בּוֹ

כְּדַאי שֶׁיֵּלֵךְ לְאַט
שֶׁלֹּא יַחְשְׁבוּ עָלָיו
שֶׁהוּא מְמַהֵר לְהַשִּׂיג כְּמִיהוֹתָיו

הוּא תָּמִיד
נוֹשֵׂא עִמּוֹ שִׁיר
וּמַה יַּעֲשֶׂה לוֹ הַשִּׁיר שֶׁהוּא מֵכִיל

הַשִּׁיר מְשַׁכֵּךְ אֶת תַּאֲוָתוֹ לְרִיצָה לְמֶרְחַקִּים

וְעָלָיו לָדַעַת
שֶׁגַּם אִם יַעֲמֹד מִלֶּכֶת
הוּא יַגִּיעַ

מִפְּנֵי שֶׁהוּא תָּמִיד
בְּאֶמְצַע יְרוּשָׁלַיִם

In the Sealed Rooms[23]

Within the great fear
we rubbed against each other
to feel warmth
to feel children.
In the sealed rooms
we were all children.

In the sealed rooms
there was no air
in the sealed rooms
we nourished ourselves
with the air within us.

---

[23]During the Gulf War (1991) Saddam Hussein threatened to attack Israel, and rooms had to be sealed to protect against chemical weapons. (Author's note.)

בחדרים האטומים

בְּתוֹךְ הַפַּחַד הַגָּדוֹל
הִתְחַכַּכְנוּ זֶה בָּזֶה
לְהַרְגִּישׁ חֹם
לְהַרְגִּישׁ יְלָדִים.
בַּחֲדָרִים הָאֲטוּמִים
הָיִינוּ כֻּלָּנוּ יְלָדִים.

בַּחֲדָרִים הָאֲטוּמִים
לֹא הָיָה אֲוִיר
בַּחֲדָרִים הָאֲטוּמִים
כִּלְכַּלְנוּ אֶת עַצְמֵנוּ
בָּאֲוִיר שֶׁהָיָה בְּתוֹכֵנוּ.

Cesspits

With her fingernails my mother
dug up the earth
down to the cesspits
she had no bomb shelter in the house
and throughout her life
from war to war
and throughout her life
from cesspit to cesspit

ספיגה

אִמִּי חָפְרָה בְּצִפָּרְנֶיהָ
בָּאֲדָמָה
אֶל בּוֹרוֹת הַסְּפִיגָה
כִּי מִקְלָט לֹא הָיָה לָהּ בַּבַּיִת
וְכָל חַיֶּיהָ
מִמִּלְחָמָה לְמִלְחָמָה
וְכָל חַיֶּיהָ
מִסְּפִיגָה לִסְפִיגָה

The Poetry of 1991

Six-year-old Shlomit
then drew a child's circle
and said:
No rockets will come in here
and neither will Saddam.
My six-year-old daughter Shlomit
would purify air
in small nylon bags
in paper bags
repelling rockets
in circles upon circles
drawn with a child's chalk.

שירת 1991

שְׁלוֹמִית בַּת הַשֵּׁשׁ
עָגָה אָז עִגּוּל שֶׁל יְלָדִים,
וְהָיְתָה אוֹמֶרֶת
כָּאן לֹא יַעַבְרוּ טִילִים
לֹא יַעֲבֹר סָדָאם.
שְׁלוֹמִית בִּתִּי בַּת הַשֵּׁשׁ
הָיְתָה מְטַהֶרֶת אֲוִיר
בְּבַנְיָלוֹנִים קְטַנִּים
בְּשַׂקִּיּוֹת שֶׁל נְיָר
הָיְתָה הוֹדֶפֶת טִילִים
בְּעִגּוּלִים עִגּוּלִים
שֶׁל גִּיר שֶׁל יְלָדִים.

Our Pain at Night

Our pain comes upon us at night
stealthily, plotting quietly
like trickling waters
our pain comes upon us at night
when all are asleep

Eternal sentries
we drift
between wakefulness and sleep
and memory visits us
like a malevolent friend

To sleep just once
the sleep of infants till morning

מכאובינו בלילה

מַכְאוֹבֵינוּ בָּאִים עָלֵינוּ בַּלַּיְלָה
בְּהֶחָבֵא, בִּמְזִמָּה שְׁקֵטָה
כְּמוֹ מַיִם מְחַלְחֲלִים
בָּא עָלֵינוּ מַכְאוֹבֵנוּ בַּלַּיְלָה
כְּשֶׁכֻּלָּם יְשֵׁנִים

אֲנַחְנוּ בְּנִים לֹא נִים
בֵּין עֵרוּת לְשֵׁנָה
אֲנַחְנוּ הַשּׁוֹמְרִים הַנִּצְחִיִּים
הַזִּכָּרוֹן פּוֹקֵד אוֹתָנוּ
כְּמוֹ חָבֵר רַע

רַק פַּעַם אַחַת לִישֹׁן
שְׁנַת תִּינוֹקוֹת עַד הַבֹּקֶר

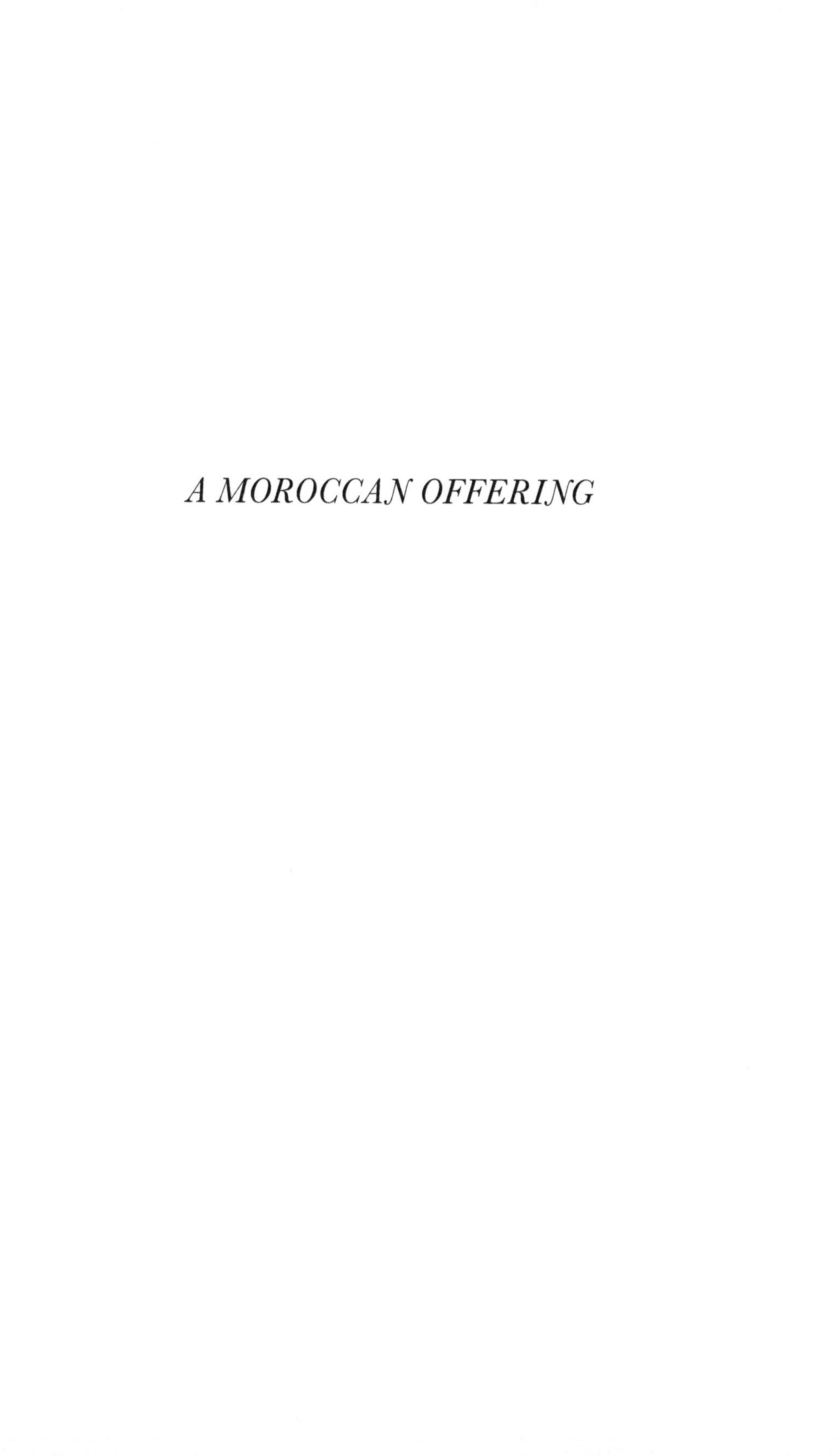

A MOROCCAN OFFERING

Preliminary Background Words

My mother my mother
from a village of shrubs green of a different green.
From a bird's nest producing milk sweeter than sweet.
From a nightingale's cradle of a thousand Arabian nights.

My mother my mother
who staved off evil
with her middle fingers
with beating her chest
on behalf of all mothers.

My father my father
who delved into worlds
who sanctified the Sabbath with pure arak
who was most practiced
in synagogue traditions.

And I and I
having distanced myself
deep into my heart
would recite
when all were asleep
short Bach masses
deep into my heart
in Jewish-
Moroccan.

דברי רקע ראשוניים

אִמִּי אִמִּי
מִכְּפַר הַשִּׂיחִים הַיְרֻקִּים בְּיָרֹק אַחֵר.
מִקַּן הַצִּפּוֹרִים הַמַּחְלִיבוֹת חָלָב מָתוֹק מִכָּל מָתוֹק,
מֵעֶרֶשׂ זְמִירֵי אֶלֶף לַיְלָה וְעוֹד לַיְלָה.

אִמִּי אִמִּי
שֶׁהִרְחִיקָה רָעוֹת
בְּאֶצְבָּעוֹת צְרֵדוֹת
בְּהַלְקָאוֹת חָזֶה
וּבְשֵׁם כָּל הָאִמָּהוֹת.

אָבִי אָבִי
אֲשֶׁר עָסַק בְּעוֹלָמוֹת
אֲשֶׁר קִדֵּשׁ שַׁבָּתוֹת בְּעָרָק נָקִי
אֲשֶׁר הָיָה בָּקִי מֵאֵין כָּמוֹהוּ
בְּהִלְכוֹת בֵּית כְּנֶסֶת.

אֲנִי אֲנִי
שֶׁהִרְחַקְתִּי עַצְמִי
הַרְחֵק אֶל תּוֹךְ לִבִּי
שֶׁכְּשֶׁהַכֹּל הָיוּ יְשֵׁנִים
הָיִיתִי מְשַׁנֵּן
הַרְחֵק אֶל תּוֹךְ לִבִּי
מִסּוֹת קְטַנּוֹת שֶׁל בַּךְ
בִּיהוּדִית
מָרוֹקָאִית.

Zohra El Fassia[24]

Zohra El Fassia
a singer at the court of King Muhammad the Fifth in Rabat,
    Morocco.
It is said that when she sang
soldiers drew knives
to push through the crowds
and touch the hem of her dress
kiss her fingertips
express their thanks with a rial coin.
Zohra El Fassia.
These days she can be found in Ashkelon,
in the poor section of Atikot C,
near the welfare office,
the odor of leftover sardine tins
on a wobbly three-legged table,
splendid kingly rugs stacked on a Jewish Agency bed,
and she, clad in a fading housecoat,
lingers for hours before the mirror
wearing cheap makeup,
and when she says: "Muhammad the Fifth, apple of our eyes"
it takes a moment before you understand.

Zohra El Fassia has a husky voice,
a pure heart, and eyes
awash with love.
Zohra El Fassia.

---

[24]Zorha El Fassia (1907–1994). A Jewish-Moroccan singer, she immigrated to Israel in 1962.

שיר זוהרה אלפסִיָה

זָהֲרָה אַלְפַסִיָה
זַמֶּרֶת הֶחָצֵר אֵצֶל מֻחַמַּד הַחֲמִישִׁי בְּרַבַּת שֶׁבְּמָרוֹק.
אוֹמְרִים עָלֶיהָ שֶׁכַּאֲשֶׁר שָׁרָה,
לָחֲמוּ חַיָּלִים בְּסַכִּינִים
לְפַלֵּס דֶּרֶךְ בֶּהָמוֹן
לְהַגִּיעַ אֶל שׁוּלֵי שִׂמְלָתָהּ
לְנַשֵּׁק אֶת קְצוֹת אֶצְבְּעוֹתֶיהָ
לָשִׂים כֶּסֶף רִיאָל לְאוֹת תּוֹדָה.
זָהֲרָה אַלְפַסִיָה.
הַיּוֹם, נִתָּן לִמְצֹא אוֹתָהּ
בְּאַשְׁקְלוֹן, בְּעַתִּיקוֹת ג׳, לְיַד לִשְׁכַּת הַסַּעַד,
רֵיחַ שְׁיָרִים שֶׁל קֻפְסוֹת סַרְדִּינִים
עַל שֻׁלְחָן מִתְנוֹדֵד בֶּן שָׁלוֹשׁ רַגְלַיִם,
שְׁטִיחֵי מֶלֶךְ מַרְהִיבִים, מְרֻבָּבִים עַל מִטַּת סוֹכְנוּת,
וְהִיא בַּחֲלוּק בֹּקֶר בָּהוּי
שָׁעוֹת בַּמַּרְאָה
בְּצִבְעֵי אִפּוּר זוֹלִים
וּכְשֶׁהִיא אוֹמֶרֶת:
מֻחַמַּד הַחֲמִישִׁי אִישׁוֹן עֵינֵינוּ
אֵינְךָ מֵבִין בָּרֶגַע הָרִאשׁוֹן.

לְזָהֲרָה אַלְפַסִיָה קוֹל צָרוּד,
לֵב צָלוּל וְעֵינַיִם שְׂבֵעוֹת אַהֲבָה.
זָהֲרָה אַלְפַסִיָה.

A Marginal Boy and a Social Worker

Take notice,
this is not speaking in flowers
or in hymns
or in angels.

You noticed,
I couldn't speak.
I turned mute in the proximity of your scent,
wafting slow and patient.
Mute, I would imagine your hand,
small European bird.

Take notice,
I followed you
ever since I became self-aware.
You were always levelheaded
driving me to distraction.
But now my hand reaches,
now I'm drawn in soft lines,
in the proper scent.

Now I am even wiser than you,
small European bird,
in the Middle East
you are my Solveig.

שיר נער שוליים ועובדת סוציאלית

שִׂימִי לֵב,
זֶה לֹא לְדַבֵּר בִּפְרָחִים
וְלֹא בִּזְמִירִים
וְלֹא בְּמַלְאָכִים.

שַׂמְתְּ לֵב,
לֹא יָכֹלְתִּי לְדַבֵּר.
דּוּמָם הָיִיתִי בְּטְוַח רֵיחֵךְ הַמְפַכְפֵּךְ סַבְלָנִי לְאַט,
דּוּמָם הָיִיתִי מְדַמֶּה אֶת יָדֵךְ,
צִפּוֹר אֵירוֹפֵּאִית קְטַנָּה.

שִׂימִי לֵב,
עָקַבְתִּי אַחֲרַיִךְ
מֵאָז עָמַדְתִּי עַל דַּעְתִּי
אַתְּ הָיִית עִקְבִית
עַד טֵרוּף-הַדַּעַת.
וְעַכְשָׁו יָדִי מַגַּעַת,
עַכְשָׁו אֲנִי רָשׁוּם בַּקַּוִּים הָרַכִּים
בָּרֵיחַ הַנָּכוֹן.

עַכְשָׁו אֲנִי אֲפִלּוּ חָכָם מִמֵּךְ,
צִפּוֹר אֵירוֹפֵּאִית קְטַנָּה,
בַּמִּזְרָח הַתִּיכוֹן,
אַתְּ סוֹלְוֵיג שֶׁלִּי.

Elegies for ben Shushan[25]

1.
Don't take it to heart, ben Shushan,
and if you stick a finger between your teeth
no one, frankly, will take notice,
she won't keep her fingers crossed for you
as you travel to the remote regions of sorrow,
don ben Juan
indeed ben Juan
you'd better begin to plan the truly great laugh
and a finger and a finger and a finger
in the prophetic eye
ben Shushan.

2.
Ayima leziza diali[26]
look and see
how even the sun stays away so as not to touch me,
how the birds from the treetops point their beaks at me,
how the children cast glances of fear at me,
in spite of the prison bars.

My dear mother,
it is not the chains that weigh me down,
it is my heart that's weightier than chains,
and the darkness all around is hard to bear,
my dear mother.

---

[25] A central figure in Jewish-Algerian folk tales. It is told that he killed his beloved after she had left him. While incarcerated in Oran, Algeria, he composed one of the most beautiful lamentations of the genre. (Author's note.)

[26] Moroccan Arabic: "My dear mother." Here and elsewhere, Bitton transliterates the Arabic into Hebrew and provides the Hebrew translation in parentheses as part of the poem.

אלגיות בן שושן

א.
אַל תִּקַּח לַלֵּב בֶּן שׁוּשָׁן
וְאִם תָּשִׂים אֶצְבַּע בְּשִׁנֶּיךָ
בֶּאֱמֶת מִי יָשִׂים עָלֶיךָ
הִיא לֹא תַּחְזִיק לְךָ אֶצְבָּעוֹת
בַּמַּסָּעוֹת לַפַּרְבָּרִים הַנִּדָּחִים שֶׁל הַיָּגוֹן,
דּוֹן בֶּן חוּחַן
לָכֵן בֶּן חוּחַן
תַּתְחִיל לְתַכְנֵן אֶת הַצְּחוֹק הַגָּדוֹל בֶּאֱמֶת
וְאֶצְבַּע וְאֶצְבַּע וְאֶצְבַּע
בְּעֵין הָרוּחַ
בֶּן שׁוּשָׁן.

ב.
אַיִמָּה לֶעְזִיזָה דִּיאָלִי
(בְּעַרְבִית מָרוֹקָאִית: אִמָּא יְקָרָה שֶׁלִּי.)
תִּרְאִי
אֵיךְ גַּם הַשֶּׁמֶשׁ מַרְחִיקָה שֶׁלֹּא לָגַעַת בִּי,
אֵיךְ הַצִּפּוֹרִים מֵרָאשֵׁי הָעֵצִים מְזַקְּרוֹת מַקּוֹר נֶגְדִּי,
אֵיךְ הַיְלָדִים מְיַדִּים מַבָּטִים שֶׁל פַּחַד
עַל-אַף הַסּוֹרְגִים.

אִמָּא יְקָרָה שֶׁלִּי,
זֶה לֹא הַכְּבָלִים שֶׁמַּכְבִּידִים,
זֶה לִבִּי שֶׁכָּבֵד מִכְּבָלִים,
וְהַחֹשֶׁךְ מִסָּבִיב קָשֶׁה,
אִמָּא יְקָרָה שֶׁלִּי.

A Purchase on Dizengov[27]

I purchased a store on Dizengov
to strike roots
to purchase roots
to find me a perch in Roval[28]
but
the people in Roval
I ask myself
who are these people in Roval
what's so special about these people in Roval
what makes them tick these people in Roval
I don't address the people in Roval
and when the people in Roval address me
I pull out the language,
clean words,
a most up-to-date Hebrew,
Yes, sir,
Welcome, sir,
and here the buildings loom over me
they tower over me
and here the open entryways
are inaccessible to me
here.
At nightfall
in the store on Dizengov
I pack my things
to go back to the outskirts
to the other Hebrew.

---

[27]Dizengoff Street. The deliberate misspelling alludes to the prevalent Ashkenazi prejudices in the 1950s, 60s, and 70s, targeting immigrants from N. Africa and mocking their accents.

[28]A European-style café of the period, on Dizengoff Street, known for its pastries.

שיר קנייה בדיזנגוב

קָנִיתִי חֲנוּת בְּדִיזֶנְגּוֹב
כְּדֵי לְהַכּוֹת שֹׁרֶשׁ
כְּדֵי לִקְנוֹת שֹׁרֶשׁ
כְּדֵי לִמְצֹא מָקוֹם בְּרוֹוָל
אֲבָל
הָאֲנָשִׁים בְּרוֹוָל
אֲנִי שׁוֹאֵל אֶת עַצְמִי
מִי הֵם הָאֲנָשִׁים בְּרוֹוָל,
מַה יֵּשׁ בָּאֲנָשִׁים בְּרוֹוָל,
מַה הוֹלֵךְ בָּאֲנָשִׁים בְּרוֹוָל,
אֲנִי לֹא פּוֹנֶה לָאֲנָשִׁים בְּרוֹוָל
כְּשֶׁהָאֲנָשִׁים בְּרוֹוָל פּוֹנִים אֵלַי
אֲנִי שׁוֹלֵף אֶת הַשָּׂפָה
מִלִּים נְקִיּוֹת,
כֵּן אֲדוֹנִי,
בְּבַקָּשָׁה אֲדוֹנִי,
עִבְרִית מְעֻדְכֶּנֶת מְאוֹד,
וְהַבָּתִּים הָעוֹמְדִים כָּאן עָלַי
גְּבוֹהִים כָּאן עָלַי,
וְהַפְּתָחִים הַפְּתוּחִים כָּאן
בִּלְתִּי חֲדִירִים לִי כָּאן.
בְּשָׁעָה אַפְלוּלִית
בַּחֲנוּת בְּדִיזֶנְגּוֹב
אֲנִי אוֹרֵז חֲפָצִים
לַחֲזֹר לַפַּרְבָּרִים
לָעִבְרִית הָאַחֶרֶת.

Moroccan Wedding

1.
He who hasn't seen a Moroccan wedding—
we've heard, we've heard.
Sarah daughter of Dodo,
blessed the arc of your hands over the tam-tam drums,
from one end of the village to the other
Arabs and Jews we will come.
We've seen, we've seen
the casks of arak, the links of baked pigeons,
the seven kinds of dates laid out
at the door of the house,
the proud jugs of olives,
blessed the arc of your hands over the tam-tam drums,
Sarah daughter of Dodo,
Arabs and Jews we will come
our heart slowly expands and our spirit is joyous.

2.
Ayima
ten birds want to break away from my ribcage,
my love, love of my soul,
you're like the Buskri date,
the sweetest of all,
your lips two Buskri dates
the sweetest of all.
Ayima
I bear the light of this evening
like the weight of ineffable bliss.
Ayima
I feel as though the earth is two amot[29] shorter than me,

---

[29]Plural of amah, a biblical measurement unit, the length of the forearm, from the elbow to the tip of the middle finger.

חתונה מרוקאית

א.
מִי שֶׁלֹּא רָאָה חֲתֻנָּה מָרוֹקָאִית מִיָּמָיו –
שָׁמַעְנוּ שָׁמַעְנוּ,
בְּרוּכוֹת קְמוּרוֹת יָדַיִךְ בְּתֵפֵּי הַטַּמְטַם,
שָׂרָה בַּת דּוֹדוֹ,
מִקְּצֵה הַכְּפָר וְעַד קְצֵה הַכְּפָר
עַרְבִים וִיהוּדִים נָבוֹא.
רָאִינוּ רָאִינוּ
אֶת חֶבְיוֹנִיּוֹת הָעָרָק, אֶת שַׁרְשְׁרוֹת הַיּוֹנִים הַצְּלוּיוֹת
אֶת מִרְבְּצֵי הַתְּמָרִים בְּשִׁבְעָה מִינִים
בְּפֶתַח הַבַּיִת
אֶת כַּדֵּי הַזֵּיתִים הַגֵּאִים,
בְּרוּכוֹת קְמוּרוֹת יָדַיִךְ בְּתֵפֵּי הַטַּמְטַם,
שָׂרָה בַּת דּוֹדוֹ,
עַרְבִים וִיהוּדִים נָבוֹא.
לִבֵּנוּ מִתְרַחֵב לְאַט וְנַפְשֵׁנוּ שְׂמֵחָה.

ב.
אַיִמָּה
עֶשֶׂר צִפּוֹרִים רוֹצוֹת לְהִנָּתֵק מִקְּבֹרֶת חָזִי,
יַקִּיר יַקִּיר נַפְשִׁי, כְּמוֹ תָּמָר מִסּוּג בֶּסְקְרִי
שֶׁהוּא הַסּוּג הַמָּתוֹק בְּיוֹתֵר,
שִׂפְתוֹתַיִךְ שְׁנֵי תְּמָרִים
מִסּוּג בֶּסְקְרִי שֶׁהוּא הַסּוּג הַמָּתוֹק בְּיוֹתֵר.
אַיִמָּה
אֶת אוֹר הָעֶרֶב הַזֶּה אֲנִי נוֹשֵׂא כְּמַשָּׂא הָאֹשֶׁר שֶׁלֹּא יוּשַׁר.
אַיִמָּה
אֲנִי מַרְגִּישׁ כְּמוֹ הָאָרֶץ נְמוּכָה מִמֶּנִּי שְׁתֵּי אַמּוֹת

my love, love of my soul,
your throat like a slender wrist, like the finger of fingers
bejeweled with the strings of my heart.
They will yet say: Since your wedding
there hasn't been a wedding like your wedding.

3.
I, too, want a salad of cooked pepper, first pared
then spiced with ten spices,
Mother.
I, too, want bread and a hard-boiled egg
diced and spiced with libzar and cumin.
Tum-tum-tum-tum-tum-tum
tum-tum-tum-tum-tum-tum-tum-tum-tum
on the tanbul.[30]
Nak Tehish,[31] ha-Shäyk Hassen.
Drink with me a glass of arak, Sheikh Hassen.
You shouldn't have brought all these gifts,
our dear abu[32] Mehammed.
And you who play the tanbul,
what are you doing sitting alone in the corner
while we delight in your playing.

4.
He who hasn't been to a Moroccan wedding,
he who hasn't heard Grandma Freha
trilling for the bride and groom the Maqamah of Longing,[33]
he who hasn't sat on the ground upon featherbeds and brocade
cushions,

---

[30]A small Moroccan drum
[31]Arabic blessing: May you live.
[32]Arabic: Father of.
[33]Poem of nostalgia and longing popular among Moroccan Jews.

יַקִּירָתִי יַקִּירַת נַפְשִׁי
צַוָּארֵךְ כְּמוֹ אַמַּת-יָד דַּקָּה, כְּמוֹ אֶצְבַּע הָאֶצְבָּעוֹת
עֲדוּיָה בִּרְצוּעוֹת לִבִּי.
עוֹד יֹאמְרוּ: מֵאָז חֲתֻנָּתֵךְ לֹא הָיְתָה חֲתֻנָּה כַּחֲתֻנָּתֵךְ.

ג.
גַּם אֲנִי רוֹצֶה סָלָט פִּלְפֵּל מְבֻשָּׁל שֶׁמּוֹרִידִים קֹדֶם אֶת קְלִפָּתוֹ
וּמְטַבְּלִים אוֹתוֹ בַּעֲשָׂרָה תַּבְלִינִים,
אִמָּא.
גַּם אֲנִי רוֹצֶה לַחְמָנִית עִם בֵּיצָה קָשָׁה מְרֻדֶּדֶת בְּלֶבְזָר וְקָמוּן.
תֵּה תֵּה תֵּה תֵּה תֵּה תֵּה
תֵּה תֵּה תֵּה תֵּה תֵּה תֵּה תֵּה תֵּה
בְּטַנְבּוּל.
נַק תְּעִישׁ (שֶׁתִּחְיֶה) אַשֵּׁיח חֲסֵן.
תִּשְׁתֶּה אִתִּי סֵפֶל עָרָק שֵׁיח חֲסֵן.
לֹא הָיִיתָ צָרִיךְ לְהָבִיא אֶת כָּל הַתִּקְרֹבֶת הַזֹּאת
אַבּוּ מְחַמַּד הַיָּקָר שֶׁלָּנוּ.
וְאַתָּה הַמְנַגֵּן בְּטַנְבּוּל,
מַה זֶּה הָיָה לְךָ בּוֹדֵד בַּפִּנָּה וַאֲנַחְנוּ שְׂמֵחִים בְּמַנְגִּינָתֵךְ.

ד.
מִי שֶׁלֹּא הָיָה בַּחֲתֻנָּה מָרוֹקָאִית,
מִי שֶׁלֹּא שָׁמַע אֶת סָבְתָא פְּרֶחָה
מְסַלְסֶלֶת אֶת מַקָּמַת הָעַרְגּוֹן בְּאָזְנֵי הַכַּלָּה וְהֶחָתָן,
מִי שֶׁלֹּא יָשַׁב עַל הָאָרֶץ עַל כִּסְתוֹת פּוּךְ וְכָרֵי אַטְלָס,

he who hasn't torn a chunk of bread with his hands,
he who hasn't cupped dripping salad in his palm
and washed it down with Marrakesh wine,
he who hasn't breathed in the youthful yearning of our girls,
he who hasn't been to a Moroccan wedding,
here's your ticket
come in
to stirrings in the breast
such as you have never felt.

מִי שֶׁלֹּא בָּצַע אֶת הַלֶּחֶם בִּשְׁתֵּי יָדָיו
מִי שֶׁלֹּא חָפַן בְּיָדָיו סָלָט נוֹזֵל
וְקִנַּח וְשָׁטַף אֶת פִּיו בְּיַיִן מְמֻרְקָשׁ,
מִי שֶׁלֹּא נָשַׁם אֶת הֶמְיַת הַנְּעוּרִים שֶׁל נַעֲרוֹתֵינוּ,
מִי שֶׁלֹּא הָיָה בַּחֲתֻנָּה מָרוֹקָאִית,
הִנֵּה לְךָ כַּרְטִיס
בּוֹא הִכָּנֵס
אֶל מְהוּמוֹת הֶחָזֶה
שֶׁלֹּא הֵמִיתָ אַף פַּעַם.

On the Earthquake in Agadir[34]

That night
the sky was blue in the golden valley,
the earth quiet in a lie-in-wait stillness,
and those who remember say
the air was sweet in the breast,
that it happened on a Tuesday night.
How does it happen
oh mother mother
that respectable, reasonable men
would suddenly rise, groping and shouting in the dark,
how does it happen
oh mother mother
that an entire city would suddenly rise
to grope and shout in the dark.
And afterward
oh mother mother
what does one contemplate, facing the ruins of his home,
facing the loss of his dear ones.
What is the first thing one does the morning after.

Oh mother mother
better if morning does not come.
And those who remember say that on that night
there had been such a sweet lust for sleep
it happened on a Tuesday night
oh mother.

---

[34]City in southwest Morocco. The 1960 earthquake killed thousands and is recorded as the deadliest in the history of Morocco.

על רעידת האדמה באגדיר

בָּעֶרֶב הַהוּא
הָיוּ הַשָּׁמַיִם תְּכֻלִּים בָּעֹמֶק הַמֻּזְהָב,
הָאֲדָמָה דָּמְמָה בְּשֶׁקֶט שֶׁל מַעֲרָב,
וְהַזּוֹכְרִים אוֹמְרִים
שֶׁהָאֲוִיר מָתוֹק בֶּחָזֶה,
בְּעֶרֶב יוֹם שְׁלִישִׁי זֶה הָיָה.
אֵיךְ קוֹרֶה
הוֹי אִמָּא אִמָּא
שֶׁאֲנָשִׁים מְכֻבָּדִים, מְיֻשָּׁבִים בְּדַעְתָּם
יָקוּמוּ בְּאַחַת לְגַשֵּׁשׁ בִּזְעָקוֹת בַּחֹשֶׁךְ,
אֵיךְ קוֹרֶה
הוֹי אִמָּא אִמָּא
שֶׁעִיר שְׁלֵמָה תָּקוּם בְּאַחַת
לְגַשֵּׁשׁ בִּזְעָקוֹת בַּחֹשֶׁךְ.
וְאַחַר כָּךְ
הוֹי אִמָּא אִמָּא
מַה חוֹשֵׁב הַיּוֹשֵׁב מוּל שְׁאֵרִיּוֹת בֵּיתוֹ
מוּל חֶסֶר יַקִּירָיו
מָה הַדָּבָר הָרִאשׁוֹן שֶׁיַּעֲשֶׂה בְּאוֹתוֹ בֹּקֶר.

הוֹי אִמָּא אִמָּא
וּלְוַאי וְלֹא בָּא בֹּקֶר
וְהַזּוֹכְרִים אוֹמְרִים כִּי בָּעֶרֶב הַהוּא
הָיְתָה תַּאֲוָה מְתוּקָה לְשֵׁנָה
בְּעֶרֶב יוֹם שְׁלִישִׁי זֶה הָיָה
הוֹי אִמָּא.

Meeting

Hand in hand
thirty degrees Celsius at the most
and already your blood pressure rises notably.
You peck at the beautiful words
believing, for some reason, you'll never meet again,
nearly forgetting that as soon as tomorrow,
on the bus, or in the store—
and you venture a smile, in any case,
wishing to gain time,
maybe a joke,
maybe a well-made tale,
after all, you've come polished and well-prepared,
and the tones
and the fingers
all in the right place,
and yet, this pressure in the chest,
and yet, the sweat across the face,
and later, apart, you recite fluently by heart
what you should have said this morning,
tallying, as with small change,
costing yourself dearly.

פְּגִישָׁה

יָד בְּיָד
שְׁלוֹשִׁים מַעֲלוֹת צֶלְזְיוּס לְכָל הַיּוֹתֵר
וּכְבָר לַחַץ הַדָּם עוֹלֶה בִּמְיֻחָד.
אַתָּה נוֹבֵר בַּמִּלִּים הַיָּפוֹת,
נִדְמֶה לְךָ מִשּׁוּם מָה שֶׁלֹּא תִּפָּגְשׁוּ עוֹד לְעוֹלָם,
אַתָּה כִּמְעַט שׁוֹכֵחַ שֶׁעוֹד מָחָר
בָּאוֹטוֹבּוּס אוֹ בַּחֲנוּת,
אַתָּה נוֹתֵן חִיּוּךְ עַל כָּל מִקְרֶה,
אַתָּה רוֹצֶה לְהַרְוִיחַ זְמַן,
אוּלַי בְּדִיחָה,
אוּלַי סִפּוּר מֻצְלָח,
הֲרֵי הֵכַנְתָּ הַכֹּל בְּמִצְחְצָח,
וְאֶת הַטּוֹנִים
וְאֶת הָאֶצְבָּעוֹת בַּמְּקוֹמוֹת הַנְּכוֹנִים,
וּבְכָל זֹאת הַדֹּחַק הַזֶּה בֶּחָזֶה,
וּבְכָל זֹאת הַהֲזָעָה הַזֹּאת בַּפָּנִים
וְאַחַר כָּךְ אַתָּה מְשַׁנֵּן עַל פֶּה וּבְלִי שְׁגִיאוֹת –
אֶת מַה שֶּׁהָיִיתָ צָרִיךְ לוֹמַר הַבֹּקֶר
וְאַתָּה מְפָרֵט כְּמוֹ בְּכֶסֶף קָטָן
וְאַתָּה מְשַׁלֵּם לְעַצְמְךָ בְּיֹקֶר.

THE BOOK OF NA'NA[35]

[35]Na'na: Moroccan Arabic for spearmint leaves, often used to make Moroccan mint tea.

The Love of Children in White Caftans

See here, Mother, how your birth-village turns over in me
see here how the scents gather about me
ah, the vapors of za'atar[36] in Rishon Pub in Tel Aviv
ah, the aroma of bread from the loam oven on Allenby Street.
Now an evening of a different "I" comes forth
a children's game with date pits
the love of children in white caftans
the love of children in a very old tongue:
"Inal buk"[37] "Ana huah dirbecht"[38]
You strike my sister, I'll strike yours,
You strike me, I'll strike you.
And then the sweetness of truce,
and then the heat abates in bare feet,
one by one the children disperse.

In a straw hut Jewish women toil, bringing food
in clay bowls borne on cushions,
Jewish men tell tales.
"Buya kan yekul," "Yima kant tekul"[39]
and then a quiet contentment
and then a quiet joy,
here, they've already poured the oil to appease the spirits,
all's well with the masters of the home,
here, now, sleep,
see here, Mother, how your birth-village turns in me
over a Viennese gravy.

---

[36] North-African spice.

[37] Arabic curse.

[38] Arabic: "I'm the one who won."

[39] Arabic: "Father used to say" "Mother used to say."

אהבת ילדים בְּזַרְבִּיּוֹת לבנות

הִנֵּה אֵיךְ מִתְהַפֵּךְ כְּפַר הֲלַדְתֵּךְ שֶׁבְּתוֹכִי
הִנֵּה אֵיךְ מְדַפְּקִים עָלַי הָרֵיחוֹת
אַהּ, אֵדֵי הַזַּעְתָּר בְּמַרְתֵּף רִאשׁוֹן,
אַהּ, הֶבֶל הַלֶּחֶם מִתַּנּוּר שֶׁל טִין בְּאַלֶּנְבִּי אַחַת עֶשְׂרֵה.
נֶהֱדָף אֵלַי עַכְשָׁו עֶרֶב מֵאֲנִי אַחֵר
מִשְׂחָק שֶׁל יְלָדִים בְּגַלְעִינֵי תְּמָרִים
אַהֲבַת יְלָדִים בְּזַרְבִּיּוֹת לְבָנוֹת
אַהֲבַת יְלָדִים בְּשָׂפָה זְקֵנָה מְאוֹד
"יִנְעַל בּוּק", יִנְעַל אָבִיךְ,
"אָנָא הוּאָה דִּרְבֶּחְט", אֲנִי הוּא שֶׁהִרְוַחְתִּי,
אַתָּה תַּכֶּה אֶת אֲחוֹתִי אֲנִי אַכֶּה אֶת אֲחוֹתְךָ
אַתָּה תַּכֶּה אוֹתִי אֲנִי אַכֶּה אוֹתְךָ.
וְאַחַר-כָּךְ מֶתֶק הַפִּיּוּס
וְאַחַר-כָּךְ שׁוֹכֵךְ הַחֹם בַּעֲקֵבִים יְחֵפִים,
אֶחָד-אֶחָד נוֹשְׁרִים הַיְלָדִים.

בְּבִקְתָּה שֶׁל קַשׁ נָשִׁים יְהוּדִיּוֹת מַקִּישׁוֹת, מַגִּישׁוֹת אֹכֶל בְּחֶרֶס
עַל כְּסָתוֹת, אֲנָשִׁים יְהוּדִים מַמְשִׁילִים מְשָׁלִים.
"בּוּיָה קַאן יְקוּל", אַבָּא הָיָה אוֹמֵר,
"יִמָּה קַאנְט תְּקוּל", אִמָּא הָיְתָה אוֹמֶרֶת,
וְאַחַר-כָּךְ שֹׂבַע שָׁקֵט
וְאַחַר-כָּךְ שִׂמְחָה שְׁקֵטָה,
הִנֵּה כְּבָר שָׁפְכוּ אֶת הַשֶּׁמֶן לְשַׁדֵּל אֶת הָרוּחוֹת
אֲדוֹנֵי הַבַּיִת לָהֶם הַשָּׁלוֹם,
הִנֵּה עַכְשָׁו שֵׁנָה
הִנֵּה אֵיךְ מִתְהַפֵּךְ כְּפַר הֲלַדְתֵּךְ בְּתוֹכִי, אִמִּי,
סָבִיב לְרֹטֶב וִינָאִי.

Uncle Yehuda Sharvit Between Marrakesh and Draa[40]

When my uncle Yehuda got drunk
he would dangle from the doors and walls of the hut
letting his legs hang loose
warbling all the laughter and tears inside him.
I knew he pretended to be a dimwit hiding in his drunkenness
to deliver a wisdom of wisdoms
a truth of truths
in the guise of a different person.
Today my uncle Yehuda is a name on a scroll
in a corked bottle
between beams in an attic
there in the village of Mhamid
between Marrakesh and Draa.

My aunt Sarah, Sarah daughter of Dodo,
was, it can be said, a champion tam-tam drummer.
When she drummed she stirred in the heart
a joyous apprehension fused with the setting sun.
People would stop in the field:
"Sarah daughter of Dodo is celebrating,
Sarah daughter of Dodo is celebrating."
Today my aunt Sarah is a name on a scroll
in a corked bottle
between beams in an attic
there in the village of Mhamid
between Marrakesh and Draa.
I who stand here and now
forge their names in silver and gold.

---

[40]Morocco's largest river. The region of the Draa River—the Draa Valley— in southern Morocco was home to some of the oldest Jewish communities in Morocco. The author's mother was born in the village Mhamid El Ghozlan. (Author's note.)

הדוד יהודה שרביט בין מָרָקֶשׁ לְדְרָע

כְּשֶׁדּוֹדִי יְהוּדָה הָיָה מִשְׁתַּכֵּר
הָיָה נִתְלֶה בְּיָדָיו בַּמַּשְׁקוֹפִים וּבַקִּירוֹת שֶׁל הַבִּקְתָּה
הָיָה מְדַלְדֵּל אֶת רַגְלָיו
וּמְגַרְגֵּר אֶת כָּל הַצְּחוֹק וְכָל הַבֶּכִי שֶׁבְּתוֹכוֹ.
יָדַעְתִּי עָלָיו שֶׁהוּא מִתְחַזֶּה לְסָתוּם, נֶחְבָּא בְּשִׁכְרוּתוֹ
לוֹמַר חָכְמָה שֶׁבְּחָכְמָה אֱמֶת שֶׁבֶּאֱמֶת בְּמַרְאִית שֶׁל אֲנִי אַחֵר.
הַיּוֹם, דּוֹדִי יְהוּדָה הוּא שֵׁם בְּתוֹךְ גְּוִיל
עַל פִּי בַּקְבּוּק צָרוּר בִּפְקָק
בֵּין מְרִישִׁים בַּעֲלִיַּת גַּג
שָׁם בִּכְפַר לְמְחָמֵד
בֵּין מָרָקֶשׁ לְדְרָע.

דּוֹדָתִי שָׂרָה, שָׂרָה בַּת דּוֹדוֹ,
הָיְתָה, אֶפְשָׁר לוֹמַר, אַלּוּפָה בְּתִיפּוּף בְּתֻפֵּי הַטַּמְטַם.
כְּשֶׁתּוֹפְפָה הֵקִימָה חֶרְדַּת לֵב שְׂמֵחָה
מְהוּלָה בַּשֶּׁמֶשׁ הַשּׁוֹקַעַת.
אֲנָשִׁים בְּאֶמְצַע הַשָּׂדֶה נֶעֶמְדוּ:
"שָׂרָה בַּת דּוֹדוֹ אוֹמֶרֶת חַג,
שָׂרָה בַּת דּוֹדוֹ אוֹמֶרֶת חַג".
הַיּוֹם, דּוֹדָתִי שָׂרָה הִיא שֵׁם בְּתוֹךְ גְּוִיל
עַל פִּי בַּקְבּוּק צָרוּר בִּפְקָק,
בֵּין מְרִישִׁים בַּעֲלִיַּת גַּג,
שָׁם בִּכְפַר לְמְחָמֵד בֵּין מָרָקֶשׁ לְדְרָע.
אֲנִי שֶׁעוֹמֵד עַכְשָׁו וְכָאן
רוֹקֵעַ אֶת שְׁמָם בְּכֶסֶף וּבְזָהָב.

Summary of a Conversation

What do you mean to be authentic?
To run along Dizengoff Street, shouting:
"Ana min al-Maghrib. Ana min al-Maghrib."[41]

What do you mean to be authentic?
To sit in Roval clad in my colorful Zarbia and agal,
or to publicly declaim:
Me, I am not Zohar,[42] I am Zaish, I am Zaish.[43]
And not the one, and not the other,
and still another tongue knocks in the mouth splitting the gums,
and still other odors overwhelm, treasured and repressed,
as I fall among the dialects,
lost in the medley of sounds.

---

[41]In Jewish-Moroccan: "I'm from the Atlas Mountain."

[42]Hebrew-Israeli name.

[43]A popular given name among Moroccan Jews, bearing folkloric tones. (Author's note.)

תקציר שיחה

מַה זֶה לִהְיוֹת אוֹתֶנְטִי,
לָרוּץ בְּאֶמְצַע דִּיזֶנְגוֹף וְלִצְעֹק בִּיהוּדִית מָרוֹקָאִית:
"אָנָא מֶן אֶלְמַגְרַבּ אָנָא מֶן אֶלְמַגְרַבּ"
(אֲנִי מֵהָרֵי הָאַטְלָס אֲנִי מֵהָרֵי הָאַטְלָס).

מַה זֶה לִהְיוֹת אוֹתֶנְטִי,
לָשֶׁבֶת בְּרוֹוָל בְּצִבְעוֹנִין (עֲגָאל וְזַרְבִּיָּה, מִינֵי לְבוּשׁ),
אוֹ לְהַכְרִיז בְּקוֹל: אֲנִי לֹא קוֹרְאִים לִי זֹהַר אֲנִי זַיִשׁ, אֲנִי זַיִשׁ (שֵׁם מָרוֹקָאִי).
וְזֶה לֹא, וְזֶה לֹא,
וּבְכָל זֹאת טוֹפַחַת שָׂפָה אַחֶרֶת בַּפֶּה עַד פְּקוֹעַ חֲנִיכַיִם,
וּבְכָל זֹאת תּוֹקְפִים רֵיחוֹת דְּחוּיִים וַאֲהוּבִים
וַאֲנִי נוֹפֵל בֵּין הָעֻגּוֹת
אוֹבֵד בִּבְלִיל הַקּוֹלוֹת.

Mother Is Cajoling a Bird[44]

Mother is cajoling a bird we call Timbisert
Mother is scattering seeds for a bird called Timbisert
and so, a kerchief on her head, inclined
in a bird's slant,
Mother pecks among chirps
combines signs to find traces from another place:
"Here's a straw hut,
here's a heroic girl from Arab tales,"
and so, bent, a kerchief on her head,
she's tossed from season to season with promises past.
What are you waiting for,
won't you fly,
you, heroic girl from Arab tales.

Tonight in your sleep
the kerchief of peace
the hut of peace
are for you, Mother,
and I who will remain awake,
bound to your dream through my navel,
will stand guard over a straw hut.

---

[44]When we were young, we would wait for a bird we called Timbisert. We believed that this bird, when she came, would bring good tidings from afar. When she arrived we would run to her, offer her crumbs, applaud her, and call out: "Allala Timbisert, our Lady Timbisert, what good tidings are you bringing this time?" (Author's note.)

אמי משדלת ציפור

אִמִּי מְשַׁדֶּלֶת צִפּוֹר שֶׁקּוֹרְאִים לָהּ – תִּמְבִּיסֶרְת
אִמִּי מְפַזֶּרֶת זֵרְעוֹנִים לַצִּפּוֹר שֶׁקּוֹרְאִים לָהּ תִּמְבִּיסֶרְת
כָּךְ בְּמִטְפַּחַת רֹאשׁ, רְכוּנָה,
בְּעֶמְדָּה שֶׁל צִפּוֹר
אִמִּי נוֹבֶרֶת בְּצִפְצוּפִים
מְצָרֶפֶת אוֹתוֹת לִמְצֹא עֲקֵבוֹת מִמָּקוֹם אַחֵר:
"הִנֵּה סֻכָּה שֶׁל נְצָרִים,
הִנֵּה יַלְדָּה גִּבּוֹרָה מֵעֲלִילוֹת עֶרֶב",
כָּךְ בְּמִטְפַּחַת רֹאשׁ, רְכוּנָה
נִזְרֶקֶת מֵעוֹנָה לְעוֹנָה בְּהַבְטָחוֹת עָבָר,
לָמָּה אַתְּ מַמְתִּינָה
לֹא תָּעוּפִי
יַלְדָּה גִּבּוֹרָה מֵעֲלִילוֹת עֶרֶב.

מִטְפַּחַת הַשָּׁלוֹם
סֻכַּת הַשָּׁלוֹם לָךְ אִמִּי בִּשְׁנָתֵךְ הַלַּיְלָה,
אֲנִי שֶׁאֶשָּׁאֵר עֵר
בְּטַבּוּרִי תָּפוּר לַחֲלוֹמֵךְ
שׁוֹמֵר סֻכָּה שֶׁל נְצָרִים.

Al-Keskas[45] ul-Ferran[46] 1

As soon as we arrived in the Land of Israel
my mother wished to erect her birth-village in our yard.
Bring me twigs
and I'll make you keskases
we'll sell them for one lira
or two liras
and make an honest living.
As the keskases were not sold
they were everywhere
atop the cabinets and in the drawers
on the beds and under the beds.
At times, for fun, we children would
put them atop our heads like a hat,
and, at times, in a gentle and appeasing tone
would call: Aleksikess kess kess kess

As soon as we arrived in the Land of Israel
my mother wished to erect a village in our yard.
Bring me mud
and I'll build you a ferran
and we'll set forth small breads and baked pigeons.
When the ferran had broken in half
it remained in the yard like a hump,
and we children, as birds do,
would sometimes perch on it
and sometimes shit on it or at its feet,
and sometimes, in a pampering tone,
would call: Alferiren ren ren,
and the aroma of small breads and baked pigeons
would rise in it,

---

[45]Kitchen implement made of straw, used by Moroccan Jews for the preparation of couscous.

[46]Clay oven.

אַלְקֶסְקַס אוּלְפֶרָאן (א')

כְּשֶׁרַק עָלִינוּ לְאֶרֶץ יִשְׂרָאֵל,
רָצְתָה אִמִּי לְהָקִים בַּחֲצַר הַבַּיִת כְּפַר הֲלֶדֶת.
תָּבִיאוּ לִי וְרָדִים
וַאֲנִי אֶעֱשֶׂה לָכֶם קֶסְקָסִים
וְנִמְכֹּר אוֹתָם בְּלִירָה אַחַת
אוֹ בִּשְׁתֵּי לִירוֹת
וְנִתְפַּרְנֵס בְּכָבוֹד רַב.
מִשֶּׁלֹּא נִמְכְּרוּ הַקֶּסְקָסִים
הָיוּ הַקֶּסְקָסִים בְּכָל מָקוֹם
עַל הָאֲרוֹנוֹת וּבַקַּמְטָרִים
וְעַל הַמִּטּוֹת וּמִתַּחַת לַמִּטּוֹת.
וַאֲנַחְנוּ הַיְלָדִים לִפְעָמִים בִּצְחוֹק
שָׂמִים אוֹתָם עַל הָרֹאשׁ כְּמוֹ כּוֹבַע
וְלִפְעָמִים בְּדֶרֶךְ שֶׁל עִדּוּן וּפִיּוּס
קוֹרְאִים לוֹ אַלֶקְסִיקֶס קֶס קֶס קֶס.

כְּשֶׁרַק עָלִינוּ לְאֶרֶץ יִשְׂרָאֵל,
רָצְתָה אִמִּי לְהָקִים בַּחֲצַר הַבַּיִת כְּפָר.
תְּנוּ לִי עָפָר
וַאֲנִי אֶבְנֶה לָכֶם פֶרָאן
וְנִהְיֶה מוֹצִיאִים מִתּוֹכוֹ לְחָמִים קְטַנִּים וְיוֹנִים צְלוּיוֹת.
מִשֶּׁנִּשְׁבַּר הַפֶּרָאן לְחֶצְיוֹ
נִשְׁאַר הַפֶּרָאן כְּמוֹ גִּבְעַת בַּחֲצַר הַבַּיִת,
וַאֲנַחְנוּ הַיְלָדִים כְּדַרְכָּם שֶׁל צִפּוֹרִים
לִפְעָמִים יוֹשְׁבִים עָלָיו
וְלִפְעָמִים מְחַרְבְּנִים עָלָיו וּלְרַגְלָיו
וְלִפְעָמִים בְּדֶרֶךְ שֶׁל פִּנּוּק קוֹרְאִים לוֹ: אַלֶפְרִירֶן רֶן רֶן.
וּמְרִיחִים בּוֹ לְחָמִים קְטַנִּים וְיוֹנִים צְלוּיוֹת

and sometimes I would say to her, to Mother:
Allala Smecha,[47]
why didn't you think to bring a village on your back,
now, where are you and where's the soil of the Land of Israel.[48]

[47]Arabic: "Madam Simcha."

[48]The bitter-ironic Hebrew construction, "Where are you and where," may be loosely translated as "Now where are you and where are your dreams" or "Now look at you and look at your dreams."

וַאֲנִי לִפְעָמִים אוֹמֵר לָהּ לְאִמָּא
אַלַלָּה שְׂמֵחָה (גְּבֶרֶת שִׂמְחָה)
אִם כָּךְ לָמָּה לֹא הֵבֵאת כְּפָר עַל גַּבֵּךְ
וְאֵיפֹה אַתְּ וְאֵיפֹה עֲפַר אֶרֶץ יִשְׂרָאֵל.

Al-Keskas ul-Ferran 2

And my father used to say:
Better half a house in the Land of Israel
than many beautiful homes avroad.[49]
Later he was sent to clean latrines in Beit Nabala.
Later he would stomp around with a hoe
over a plot of seedlings.
Later he began to detect the odor of strangers
wafting from the soil and the trees.
Later he began to hear the language of strangers
coming at him from people.
And I, during moments of teasing and appeasing,
would say to him:
Ewa Babba Yosef,[50]
they have hurled a tallit in your face,
and now, where are you and where's the Land of Israel.

---

[49]Abroad. Unlike "Dizengov" (note 27), here the accent and pronunciation of the father is simply rendered.

[50]Arabic: And so, Mister Yosef.

אַלְקֶסְקַס אוּלְפֶּרָאן (ב')

וְאִלּוּ אַבָּא שֶׁלִּי הָיָה אוֹמֵר:
טוֹב חֲצִי בַּיִת בְּאֶרֶץ יִשְׂרָאֵל
מֵהַרְבֵּה בָּתִּים טוֹבִים וְיָפִים בְּחוּצָה לָאָרֶס.
לְיָמִים שָׁלְחוּ אוֹתוֹ לְנַקּוֹת מַחְרָאוֹת בְּבֵית נַבַּאלָה,
לְיָמִים הָיָה מְקַרְטֵעַ עִם מַכּוֹשׁ אוֹ טוּרִיָּה
מִסָּבִיב לְגֻמָּה שֶׁל שְׁתִילִים,
לְיָמִים הִתְחִיל לְהָרִיחַ מִן הָאֲדָמָה וּמִן הָעֵצִים רֵיחַ שֶׁל גּוֹי,
לְיָמִים הִתְחִילָה לָבוֹא אֵלָיו מִן הָאֲנָשִׁים שָׂפָה שֶׁל גּוֹי,
וַאֲנִי בִּרְגָעִים שֶׁל קִנְטוּר וּפִיּוּס אוֹמֵר לוֹ:
אֶוּוֶה בָּבָּה יוֹסֵף (נוּ נוּ אָדוֹן יוֹסֵף)
הֵטִיחוּ טַלִּית בְּפָנֶיךָ
וְאֵיפֹה אַתָּה וְאֵיפֹה אֶרֶץ יִשְׂרָאֵל.

At the Feet of the Women

Who would redeem your infertility, Allala Yisha bint[51] Massouda,
a withering woman, squat, whose home is one room,
one tree, an old husband,
and whose entire life revolves around spices,
pepper and cumin and caraway and libzar,
and whose sole concern is a cooked dish
that has turned out well, or has burned.
I loved her invectives against fecund women:
They birth them in multiples of seven,
like litters of blind kittens,
they feed them straw and hide them in hay.
And my mother stands with her, soothing her:
It's not your fault, Allala Yisha,
it's the old husband you took.
And I am nine or ten years old,
a boy in whose palm you place a fistful of dates,
seat him on a stool in the sun at the feet of the women
and forget about him,
and I, listening and not listening,
get to know the ways of women,
and all the goings on in the quarter of Bnei Mellal.

Allala Yisha Allala Yisha,
now I'll divulge for you the rumors
the children whispered behind your back:
Here's the one whose baby died in her belly,
and they said the women would spit at your heels:
Tfu, Allah y setter,[52]
and warn their kids not to touch you.
But I remember, Allala Yisha,
the goodness of your hand, capping my forlorn head
on a stool in the sun.

---

[51]Arabic: Daughter of.

[52]Arabic: May Allah preserve us.

למרגלות הנשים

מִי יִפְדֶּה אֶת עֲקָרוּתֵךְ אַלָּלָה עִישָׁה בִּנְתְּ מַסְעוּדָה
אִשָּׁה עֲשֵׁשָׁה, מְרֻבַּעַת, שֶׁכָּל בֵּיתָהּ קִיטוֹן וְעֵץ אֶחָד וּבַעַל זָקֵן
שֶׁכָּל חַיֶּיהָ בְּתַבְלִינִים, בְּפִלְפֵּל וּבְקָמוּן וּבְקַרְוִיאָה וּבְלֶבְזָר,
וְשֶׁכָּל מַשָּׂאָהּ וּמַתָּנָהּ בְּתַבְשִׁיל שֶׁעָלָה בְּטוֹב אוֹ תַּבְשִׁיל שֶׁהִקְדִּיחַ.
אֲנִי אָהַבְתִּי אֶת מַעֲנֶה לְשׁוֹנָהּ בַּנָּשִׁים הַוַּלְדָנִיּוֹת:
יוֹלְדוֹת אוֹתָם שִׁבְעָה שִׁבְעָה
כְּמוֹ עֵדָה שֶׁל חֲתַלְתּוּלִים עִוְּרִים
מַאֲכִילוֹת אוֹתָם בְּקַשׁ וְטוֹמְנוֹת אוֹתָם בְּתֶבֶן.
וְאִמִּי עוֹמֶדֶת עָלֶיהָ מְרַכֶּכֶת:
זֶה לֹא מִמֵּךְ אַלָּלָה עִישָׁה,
זֶה מִזֶּה שֶׁלָּקַחְתְּ לָךְ בַּעַל זָקֵן,
וַאֲנִי בֶּן תֵּשַׁע אוֹ עֶשֶׂר,
יֶלֶד שֶׁנּוֹתְנִים חֹפֶן שֶׁל תְּאֵנִים בְּיָדוֹ
וּמוֹשִׁיבִים אוֹתוֹ עַל שְׁרַפְרַף בַּשֶּׁמֶשׁ
לְמַרְגְּלוֹת הַנָּשִׁים
וְשׁוֹכְחִים אוֹתוֹ
וַאֲנִי שׁוֹמֵעַ וְלֹא שׁוֹמֵעַ וְיוֹדֵעַ אֶת דֶּרֶךְ הַנָּשִׁים
וְכָל הַבָּא וְהוֹלֵךְ בְּרֹבַע בְּנֵי מְלָל.

לַלָּה עִישָׁה לַלָּה עִישָׁה,
עַכְשָׁו אֲנִי אַסְגִּיר אֵלַיִךְ אֶת הַשְּׁמוּעוֹת
שֶׁהַיְלָדִים מֵאֲחוֹרֵי גַּבֵּךְ הִתְלַחֲשׁוּ:
הִנֵּה הַזֹּאת שֶׁיֶּלֶד מֵת בְּתוֹךְ בִּטְנָהּ,
שֶׁהַנָּשִׁים הָיוּ יוֹרְקוֹת בַּעֲקֵבַיִךְ: טְפוּ, אַלְלָה יִסְתֶּר (אֱלֹהִים יִשְׁמֹר)
וּמַזְהִירוֹת אֶת יַלְדֵיהֶן מִלָּגַעַת בָּךְ.
אֲנִי זוֹכֵר לָךְ אַלָּלָה עִישָׁה
אֶת חֶסֶד יָדֵךְ עַל רֹאשִׁי הֶעָזוּב עַל שְׁרַפְרַף בַּשֶּׁמֶשׁ.

Zaish

Ah, beautiful old castoffs concealed among yellowing grass,
ah, small souvenirs in my blood
small anchors of my life
to keep me from suddenly rising now
to fly away and vanish.

Come, my Zaish, to lead me away with a gentle hand
toward an enduring delight of no future no past
in this very picture a familiar face
familiar homes familiar familiars
to be and to be in the familiar places.

You the most loyal among my friends
together we'll go searching for discarded iron scraps
to make a kick scooter and go fast fast down the street
before the astonished eyes of mothers.

We'll go searching for half a lira or even a lira
and only we will spot it
hiding among feet
and no one notices it
and later only you and I will spend it
on a sticky candy, sweet and syrupy on cheek and chin,
you and I who used to steal fleeting sights in forbidden yards.

How satisfying they were the petty flare-ups
here, here, you and I and "Yahu" wouldn't speak an entire year
except through "tell him," exchanging between us the most
    prized gifts:
Tell him to give me ten apricot pits
and in exchange I'll give him a small magnet
that distinguishes good copper from a piece of junk.

זַיִשׁ

אַהּ, גְרוּטָאוֹת יָפוֹת חֲבוּיוֹת בֵּין עֲשָׂבִים מַצְהִיבִים,
אַהּ, מַזְכָּרוֹת קְטַנּוֹת שֶׁבְּדָמִי
עֲגָנִים קְטַנִּים שֶׁל חַיַּי
שֶׁלֹּא אָקוּם פִּתְאוֹם עַכְשָׁו וְאָעוּף וְאֵינֶנִּי.

בּוֹא זַיִשׁ שֶׁלִּי שֶׁתּוֹבִיל אוֹתִי בְּיָד קַלָּה
אֶל חֶמְדָּה מִתְמַשֶּׁכֶת בְּלִי עָתִיד בְּלִי עָבָר
בְּעֶצֶם הַתְּמוּנָה הַזֹּאת פָּנִים מֻכָּרוֹת
בָּתִּים מֻכָּרִים מֻכָּרִים מֻכָּרִים
לִהְיוֹת וְלִהְיוֹת בַּמְּקוֹמוֹת הַמֻּכָּרִים.

אַתָּה הַנֶּאֱמָן בַּחֲבֵרַי נֵצֵא לְחַפֵּשׂ בַּרְזִלִּים זְרוּקִים
לַעֲשׂוֹת קוֹרְקִינֶט שֶׁנִּהְיֶה רָצִים רָצִים בְּמוֹרַד הָרְחוֹב
לְעֵינֵי אִמָּהוֹת מִתְפַּלְּאוֹת.

נֵצֵא לְחַפֵּשׂ חֲצִי לִירָה אוֹ אֲפִלּוּ לִירָה אַחַת
וְרַק אֲנַחְנוּ נָשִׂים לֵב אֵלֶיהָ
חֲבוּיָה בֵּין רַגְלַיִם
וְאֵין אִישׁ מַבְחִין בָּהּ
וְאַחַר כָּךְ רַק אֲנַחְנוּ נִקְנֶה אוֹתָהּ כֻּלָּהּ
מַמְתָּק דָּבִיק נִתְפָּשׂ מָתוֹק מָתוֹק בַּלֶּחִי וּבַסַּנְטֵר,
אַתָּה וַאֲנִי הָיִינוּ גּוֹנְבִים מַרְאוֹת חֲטוּפִים בַּחֲצֵרוֹת אֲסוּרוֹת.

מַה נָּעֲמוּ הָרֶגְזוֹת הַקְּטַנּוֹת
הִנֵּה הִנֵּה אַתָּה וַאֲנִי וְ"יַהוּ" שָׁנָה שְׁלֵמָה לֹא דִּבַּרְנוּ
רַק בְּ"תַגִּיד לוֹ" וּמַחֲלִיפִים בֵּינֵינוּ אֶת מֵיטַב הַמַּתָּנוֹת
תַּגִּיד לוֹ שֶׁיִּתֵּן לִי עֲשָׂרָה גַּלְעִינִים שֶׁל מִשְׁמְשִׁים
וְאֶתֵּן לוֹ בִּתְמוּרָה מַגְנֵט קָטָן
שֶׁמַּבְדִּיל בֵּין נְחֹשֶׁת טוֹבָה לִסְתָם בַּרְזֶל זָרוּק.

An entire year of clandestine love laced with mild fretting,
and, upon our return from our outings, barefoot and saturated
with colors and shapes, sated and fatigued
with the sweetness of bare feet in moist soil,
we would return in the evening, Zaish, for the day's meal,
a pot of potatoes offering a taste of heaven.
In those days, Zaish, our palates
would transform a fistful of kernels
into brilliant delights.

You, Zaish Zaish Zaish, you of the sparkling name,
you, the candle in the soft chambers inside me,
may the affirmation of a different prospect always be before me,
you who make light of my overburdened head
as you lean on one slender hand
so that I sometimes say,
Here, here, all at once everything will close in on me

I am the captive of no escape
in this place, this place

In these people, these people.

שָׁנָה שְׁלֵמָה שֶׁל אַהֲבָה נִסְתֶּרֶת יְצוּקָה בְּרֹגֶז קַל
וְאַחֲרֵי שׁוּבֵנוּ מִמַּסָּעוֹת יְחֵפִים שְׂבֵעֵי צוּרוֹת וּצְבָעִים
גְּדוּשֵׁי טְעָמִים עֲיֵפִים
מִמְּתִיקוּת רֶגֶל יְחֵפָה בָּאֲדָמָה לַחָה
נַחְזֹר זַיִשׁ לַאֲרוּחַת הַיּוֹם בָּעֶרֶב
תַּפּוּחֵי אֲדָמָה קְדֵרָה שְׁלֵמָה בְּטַעַם גַּן עֵדֶן
הַחֵךְ הַהוּא שֶׁלָּנוּ זַיִשׁ
הָיָה הוֹפֵךְ סְתָם חֹפֶן גַּרְגִּירִים
לַעֲדָנִים זוֹהֲרִים.

אַתָּה זַיִשׁ זַיִשׁ זַיִשׁ אַתָּה הַשֵּׁם הַזּוֹהֵר אַתָּה הַנֵּר
בַּמְּדוֹרִים הָרַכִּים שֶׁבְּתוֹכִי
וּלְוַאי וְתַעֲמֹד לְנֶגְדִּי תָּמִיד עֵדוּת לְאֶפְשָׁרוּת אַחֶרֶת
אַתָּה שֶׁמֵּקֵל לְרָאשֵׁי רֹאשׁ עָמוּס
נִשְׁעָן עַל יָד דַּקָּה אַחַת
שֶׁלִּפְעָמִים אֲנִי אוֹמֵר
הִנֵּה הִנֵּה יִסְגֹּר עָלַי הַכֹּל בְּאַחַת

אֲנִי הַשָּׁבוּי לְלֹא בְּרִיחָה
בַּמָּקוֹם בַּמָּקוֹם וּבָאֲנָשִׁים

בָּאֲנָשִׁים בָּאֲנָשִׁים.

Sullika's Qasida[53]

1.
Sullika, a renowned folkloric figure among Moroccan Jews,
a girl celebrated for her beauty across the land,
it is told that when her fame reached the son of the king,
Prince bin Idris,
he brought her to his palace in Rabat.

After a time she was found dead
in a canopy bed wearing all her jewels
and they say she was even more beautiful
in her death than in her life.

Ever since, many poems and tales have been written about her.

2.
I keep leafing through you and through me.
Here, on the sidewalks of Ramat-Gan, I imagine a silence
even though I know and hear the great clamor.
Like a blast your name rose in my ears
during a party with Jews of Moroccan descent,
Maakouda batata[54] and cooked pepper on the plates
and Colomber wine in the glasses
and a clean napkin across the knees.
Your name was mentioned and came to me as a blow
above the glasses, while your name, I sensed,
infused all present with tenderness and grace,
like the aroma of dessert over the conversation
around the table.
Only I felt this way—
the blood pounded in my temples,
I spilled wine on the clean napkin on my knee.

---

[53] Arabic. A form of lyric poetry.
[54] Moroccan potato cakes.

קַסִּידַת סוּלִיקָה

א.
סוּלִיקָה, דְּמוּת יְדוּעָה בַּפוֹלְקְלוֹר שֶׁל יַהֲדוּת מָרוֹקוֹ.
נַעֲרָה שֶׁנּוֹדְעָה בְּיָפְיָהּ בְּכָל הָאָרֶץ
מְסֻפָּר עָלֶיהָ, שֶׁכַּאֲשֶׁר הִגִּיעַ שִׁמְעָהּ לְבֶן הַמֶּלֶךְ
הַנָּסִיךְ בֶּן אִדְרִיס
לָקַח אוֹתָהּ לְאַרְמוֹנוֹ בְּרַבַּת

לְאַחַר זְמַן נִמְצְאָה מֵתָה
בְּתוֹךְ אַפִּרְיוֹן עֲדוּיָה כָּל עֲדָיֶיהָ
אוֹמְרִים שֶׁהָיְתָה יָפָה בְּמוֹתָהּ יוֹתֵר מִבְּחַיֶּיהָ.

מֵאָז נִכְתְּבוּ עָלֶיהָ שִׁירִים וּמַעֲשִׂיּוֹת רַבִּים.

ב.
אֲנִי חוֹזֵר וּמְדַפְדֵּף בָּהּ וּמְדַפְדֵּף בִּי,
כָּאן עַל מִדְרְכוֹת רָמַת-גַּן אֲנִי מְדַמֶּה לִי שֶׁקֶט
לַמְרוֹת שֶׁאֲנִי יוֹדֵעַ וְשׁוֹמֵעַ אֶת הָרַעַשׁ הַגָּדוֹל
כְּמוֹ מַכָּה עָלָה אָז שְׁמֵךְ בְּאָזְנַי
בִּמְסִבַּת חֶבְרֶה מָרוֹקָאִים
מַעֲקוּדָה בְּצַלַּחַת וּפִלְפֵּל מְבֻשָּׁל בְּצַלַּחַת
וְיֵין קוֹלוֹמְבֶּר בְּכוֹסוֹת
וּמַפִּית נְקִיָּה עַל הַבִּרְכַּיִם.
כְּמוֹ מַכָּה הֶעֱלוּ אָז אֶת שְׁמֵךְ
מִסָּבִיב לַכּוֹסוֹת וּשְׁמֵךְ אֲנִי הִרְגַּשְׁתִּי
מָסַךְ רַכּוּת וְיֹפִי עָדִין בָּאֲנָשִׁים
כְּמוֹ אֲרוֹמָה שֶׁל קְנוּחַ בְּשֶׁטֶף הַשִּׂיחָה
מִסָּבִיב לַשֻּׁלְחָן.
רַק אֲנִי כָּךְ הִרְגַּשְׁתִּי
עָלָה לִי הַדָּם לַמּוֹחַ,
נִשְׁפַּךְ לִי הַיַּיִן עַל הַמַּפִּית הַנְּקִיָּה
שֶׁעַל הַבִּרְכַּיִם.

And I keep leafing through you and through me,
touching-not-touching the essence of your memory across the generations.
Since the thirteenth-fourteenth century,
a mist of soft memory
barely graspable
affecting me in a good and a bad way at once
I was like a mad man at that party
drooling saliva down my chin, staining my shirt,
and disagreeable in conversation.
For me you were not the aroma of dessert
in a gathering of Moroccan friends.

3.
Zani lefrak fessbach bekri[55]
and all my relatives took cover in the walls
but I reclaimed the echo of their shadows from the walls.

Oh Mother Mother how in one morning an entire life came to an end
how my life ended in a span of a morning.

4.
You gossiping old ladies of the house
you who rubbed my feet with Marrakesh oil
give me your blessing on my way to Rabat
for the road to Rabat is the end of the road for me.

You, the girls of the *mellah*,[56]
sisters in the baking of bread in the ferran,
sisters in a game of dates in the evening,

---

[55] Arabic: The blow of separation came upon me in early morning.

[56] Walled Jewish quarter in Moroccan cities. Pronounced "melach" ("salt" in Arabic, Aramaic, and Hebrew), it possibly alludes to the task assigned to Jews to salt the severed heads of enemies, brought home as trophies by Muslim soldiers returning from battle.

וַאֲנִי חוֹזֵר וּמְדַפְדֵּף בָּךְ וּמְדַפְדֵּף בִּי
נוֹגֵעַ וְלֹא נוֹגֵעַ בְּתַמְצִית זִכְרֵךְ מֵעֵבֶר לַדּוֹרוֹת.
מִן הַמֵּאָה הַשְּׁלֹשׁ עֶשְׂרֵה הָאַרְבַּע עֶשְׂרֵה,
עָנָן שֶׁל זִכָּרוֹן רַךְ
לֹא נִתְפֶּשֶׂת יוֹתֵר מִשֶּׁנִּתְפֶּשֶׂת
וְעוֹשָׂה טוֹב וְעוֹשָׂה רַע גַּם יַחַד
בַּמְּסִבָּה הַהִיא הָיִיתִי כְּמוֹ מְשֻׁגָּע
עִם רִיר בַּסַּנְטֵר, כְּתָמִים בַּחֻלְצָה
וְלֹא נָעִים בַּשִּׂיחָה
בִּשְׁבִילִי לֹא הָיִית אֲרוּמָה לְקִנּוּחַ
שֶׁל עֶרֶב שֶׁל חֶבְרֶה מָרוֹקָאִים.

ג.
זָ'נִי לֶפְּרָק פֶּסְבָּח בֶּקְרִי
בָּאָה עָלַי מַכַּת הַפְּרִידָה הַשְׁכֵּם בַּבֹּקֶר
וְכָל קְרוֹבַי נֶחְבְּאוּ אֶל הַקִּירוֹת
אֲבָל אֲנִי אֶת הֵד צִלָּם לָכַדְתִּי מִן הַקִּירוֹת.

הַי אִמָּא אִמָּא אֵיךְ בֶּן בֹּקֶר עָבְרוּ חַיִּים שְׁלֵמִים
אֵיךְ עָבְרוּ חַיַּי בֶּן בֹּקֶר.

ד.
אַתֶּן זְקֵנוֹת הַבַּיִת הַמְהַלְּכוֹת רָכִיל
אַתֶּן שֶׁסַּכְתֶּן אֶת רַגְלַי בְּשֶׁמֶן מָרָקֶשׁ
תְּנוּ לִי בְּרָכָה בַּדֶּרֶךְ לְרַבַּת
כִּי אֵין דֶּרֶךְ מִן הַדֶּרֶךְ לְרַבַּת.

אַתֶּן נַעֲרוֹת הַמֶּלַח
אֲחָיוֹת לְמַעֲשֵׂה הַלֶּחֶם בַּפֶּרָאן,
לְמִשְׂחַק הַתְּמָרִים בָּעֶרֶב,

give me your blessing on my way to Rabat
for the road to Rabat is the end of the road for me.

May your way to Rabat be sweet,
our sister in a game of dates in the evening.
May your way to Rabat be sweet,
you who had sweetened our old eyes.
May peace be with you on your way to Rabat.

5.
Good people, give me hands to keep me from drowning
give me down cushions and silk featherbeds
to keep me warm
against the chill in my heart.

6.
In broad daylight they robbed me of your dark eyes Sullika
in broad daylight they took from me the purity of your face
    Sullika
the charm of your silhouette in the doorway Sullika
the essence of my life they wrested from me Sullika.

7.
Oh the bird of good tidings
what have you brought me this time?
For you, the bird of good tidings,
I'll bring offerings of millet grains,
here, the couscous is made and ready to be served
if you tell me where my faraway beloved is now.

My bird, my small heart,
just give me a sign
and I'll make for you a lacy garb and a caftan.
You, the bird of birds,

תְּנוּ לִי בְּרָכָה בַּדֶּרֶךְ לְרַבַּת
כִּי אֵין דֶּרֶךְ מִן הַדֶּרֶךְ לְרַבַּת.

תִּמְתַּק לָךְ דַּרְכֵּךְ בַּדֶּרֶךְ לְרַבַּת
אֲחוֹתֵנוּ לְמִשְׂחַק הַתְּמָרִים בָּעֶרֶב.
תִּמְתַּק לָךְ דַּרְכֵּךְ לְרַבַּת
אַתְּ שֶׁהִמְתַּקְתְּ אֶת עֵינֵינוּ הַזְּקֵנוֹת.
שְׂאִי שָׁלוֹם בַּדֶּרֶךְ לְרַבַּת.

ה.
תְּנוּ לִי יָדַיִם מִפְּנֵי הַטְּבִיעָה אֲנָשִׁים טוֹבִים
תְּנוּ לִי כָּרִים שֶׁל פּוּךְ
כְּסָתוֹת שֶׁל מֶשִׁי
לְהִתְחַמֵּם מִפְּנֵי הַקֹּר שֶׁבְּלִבִּי.

ו.
חָמְסוּ לִי אֶת שְׁחוֹר עֵינַיִךְ בְּאֶמְצַע הַצָּהֳרַיִם סוּלִיקָה
בְּאֶמְצַע הַצָּהֳרַיִם לָקְחוּ מִמֶּנִּי אֶת תֹּם פָּנַיִךְ
אֶת חֶמְדַּת צְדוֹדִיתֵךְ עַל סַף הַדֶּלֶת סוּלִיקָה
אֶת עֶצֶם חַיַּי גָּזְלוּ מִמֶּנִּי סוּלִיקָה.

ז.
הוֹי צִפּוֹר הַמְבַשֶּׂרֶת בְּשׂוֹרוֹת טוֹבוֹת,
מָה הֵבֵאת לִי הַפַּעַם?
אַתְּ צִפּוֹר הַמְבַשֶּׂרֶת,
אַקְרִיב לָךְ זֵרְעוֹנִים שֶׁל דֹּחַן,
הִנֵּה הַקּוּסְקוּס עָשׂוּי וּמוּכָן,
אִם תְּגַלִּי הֵיכָן אֲהוּבִי עַכְשָׁו בַּמֶּרְחַקִּים.
אַתְּ צִפּוֹר, לֵב קָטָן שֶׁלִּי,
תְּנִי לִי אוֹת וְסִימָן
וְלָךְ אָכִין
מַלְבּוּשׁ תַּחְרָה וְקַפְטָן.
אַתְּ צִפּוֹר הַצִּפּוֹרִים,

you, a glowing eye,
my love is now somewhere on a dirt road.
I'll scoop for you ladlefuls from the bowl.

8.
It's been ten years since I've seen my son
he may be in a hut in the mountains or in a remote desert
or he may have been swept in the wake of a sinking ship.
It's been ten years since I've seen my son,
my breasts have withered, my face has dried up,
my bed is made of thorns, the food in my mouth—worms.
May Allah sweeten his rest at night,
may Allah pave his way during the day.

9.
You, my beloved, are as handsome as the parochet[57] during holidays
you are the gilded teapot
at the center of the silver tray
I'm just an embroidered glass at your side
with you I'll share my bread and bed
with you I'll share my secret dream
your two eyes lighted lands.

10.
There's no better refuge than home
we will go up to the wall of the *mellah*
we will not go beyond the walls of the *mellah*.
We were born here and here we shall die,
within the walls of the *mellah*, here at home.
Here the aroma of bread in the ferran
here the touch of fabric and spindle
we will go up to the wall of the *mellah*
we will not go beyond the walls of the *mellah*.

---

[57] Curtain, customarily quite ornate, covering the Torah Ark in synagogues.

אַתְּ בָּבַת עַיִן בּוֹהֶקֶת,
אַהֲבָתִי עַכְשָׁו אֵי שָׁם בְּדֶרֶךְ עָפָר.
לָךְ אֶתֵּן מְלוֹא חָפְנַיִם מִן הַמֶּצֶקֶת.

ח.

עֶשֶׂר שָׁנִים אֶת בְּנִי שֶׁלִּי לֹא רָאִיתִי
אוּלַי בְּבִקְתָּה שָׁם בֵּין הֶהָרִים אוֹ בְּמִדְבָּר שׁוֹמֵם,
אוֹ אוּלַי נִסְחַף בֵּין הַגַּלִּים בָּאֳנִיָּה טְרוּפָה.
עֶשֶׂר שָׁנִים אֶת בְּנִי שֶׁלִּי לֹא רָאִיתִי,
שָׁדַי צָמְקוּ, יָבְשׁוּ פָּנַי,
מַצָּעַי קוֹצִים, וְהָאֹכֶל שֶׁבְּפִי – תּוֹלָעִים.
אַלְלַהּ יַנְעִים אֶת עַרְשׂוֹ בַּלַּיְלָה,
אַלְלַהּ יְסַלֵּל אֶת דַּרְכּוֹ בַּיּוֹם.

ט.

דּוֹדִי יָפֶה כְּמוֹ פָּרֹכֶת בַּחַג
אַתָּה קֻנְקַן הַתֵּה הַמֻּזְהָב בְּאֶמְצַע מַגַּשׁ הַכֶּסֶף,
אֲנִי רַק כּוֹס רְקוּמָה לְצִדְּךָ
אִתְּךָ אֶתְחַלֵּק בַּלֶּחֶם וּבַמִּטָּה,
אִתְּךָ אֶחְלֹק אֶת חֲלוֹמִי הַכָּמוּס
שְׁתֵּי עֵינֶיךָ אֲרָצוֹת מוּאָרוֹת.

י.

אֵין מִסְתּוֹר טוֹב מִן הַבַּיִת,
עַד חוֹמַת הַמֶּלַח נָבוֹא,
לֹא נַעֲבֹר אֶת חוֹמוֹת המלח.
כָּאן נוֹלַדְנוּ, כָּאן גַּם נָמוּת,
בֵּין חוֹמוֹת הַמֶּלַח כָּאן בְּתוֹךְ הַבַּיִת.
כָּאן רֵיחַ הַלֶּחֶם בַּפֶּרָאן,
כָּאן מַגַּע הַכֶּסֶת בַּכִּישׁוֹר,
עַד חוֹמַת הַמֶּלַח נָבוֹא
וְלֹא נַעֲבֹר אֶת חוֹמַת הַמֶּלַח.

11.

And you, the tree beyond my window,
blessed in your freedom
to grant love and refuge
to lost birds.
Only I lack nest and branch
to cuddle me.

יא.

וְאַתָּה, הָעֵץ שֶׁמֵּעֵבֶר לְחַלּוֹנִי,
אַשְׁרֶיךָ שֶׁאַתָּה חָפְשִׁי
לְהַעֲנִיק אַהֲבָה וּמִסְתּוֹר
לְצִפּוֹרִים תּוֹעוֹת.
רַק אֲנִי בְּלִי קֵן וּבְלִי עֲנָפִים
שֶׁיְּחַבְּקוּנִי.

INTERCONTINENTAL BIRD

To Speak Within the Light

Morning Prayer for Rabbi David Buzaglo[58]

VERSION 1

I will allow myself to say
something leapt in me when I heard your name
I will allow myself to say
the juice of my love spills over your thresholds
Rabbi David Buzaglo
come away from the corner
to the stage of stages
something leapt in me toward the echo of your intonations
following my footsteps I arrived behind you
Rabbi David Buzaglo

VERSION 2

Come away from the corner
to the stage of stages
Rabbi David Buzaglo
remembering you
my heart is a tree rooted in streams of water
following my footsteps I arrived behind you
where I found my face in your face
the name of all my dreams about you
you and I are from the bowl of honey
I met you within the light

---

[58]Rabbi David Buzaglo (1903–1975). Renowned Moroccan poet and *paytan* (liturgical poet), scholar, and cantor, Buzaglo immigrated to Israel in 1965.

לדבר בעצם הנהרה

שחרית לר' דוד בוזגלו, מגדולי פייטני יהדות מרוקו

נוסח א'

אַרְשֶׁה לְעַצְמִי לוֹמַר
מַשֶּׁהוּ בִּי נִתָּר לִשְׁמֹעַ אֶת שְׁמֶךָ
אַרְשֶׁה לְעַצְמִי לוֹמַר
עֲסִיס אֲהֲבָתִי נִגָּר עַל סַף דְּלָתֶיךָ
בּוֹא מִן הַפִּנָּה
אֶל בָּמַת הַבָּמוֹת
ר' דָּוִד בּוּזַגְלוֹ
מַשֶּׁהוּ בִּי נִתָּר אֶל הֵד צְלִילֶיךָ
כִּי בְּלֶכְתִּי אַחֲרַי הִגַּעְתִּי אַחֲרֶיךָ
ר' דָּוִד בּוּזַגְלוֹ

נוסח ב'

בּוֹא מִן הַפִּנָּה
אֶל בָּמַת הַבָּמוֹת
ר' דָּוִד בּוּזַגְלוֹ
בְּזָכְרִי אוֹתְךָ
לִבִּי עֵץ שָׁתוּל עַל פַּלְגֵי מַיִם
בְּלֶכְתִּי אַחֲרַי הִגַּעְתִּי אַחֲרֶיךָ
אָז מָצָאתִי מִפָּנַי בְּפָנֶיךָ
שֵׂם כָּל חֲלוֹמוֹתַי עָלֶיךָ
אַתָּה וַאֲנִי מְמֻצֶּקֶת הַדְּבַשׁ
אִתְּךָ נִפְגַּשְׁתִּי בְּעֶצֶם הַנְּהָרָה

In Praise of the Dreamers of Jerusalem

Humbly I bow before the splendor of your wrinkled faces,
dreamers of Jerusalem,
to celebrate the marvel of your memory revived in me.
Your names rise in me like a staff that suddenly springs blossoms.
Rabbi David Hassine[59] and your emblem nine daughters
all of them well-versed in Scripture.
And you Freha bat Yosef[60]
the whole of you a veiled bride
drumming the lines of a poem
as if with silver foot bracelets.
And you Shlomo Gozlan[61]
bartering your poetry on crossroads
balsam and cinnamon and aromatic herbs.
And I too will rejoin with a poem for you dreamers
from rosh Amanah[62] and from rosh Snir.[63]
From my daily ration and my life's foam
in me I will build for you a permanent home.

---

[59]Rabbi David Hassine (1727–1792). Considered one of the greatest Hebrew Moroccan poets. Also renowned for his liturgical poems (*piyyutim*) throughout the Mizrahi world.

[60]Hebrew poetess in eighteenth-century Morocco.

[61]Eighteenth-century Hebrew Moroccan poet of the Draa Valley.

[62] Amanah—name of a mountain. Alludes to The Song of Songs (4:8): "Tashuri m'rosh Amanah"—"Observe from the peak of Amanah."

[63]Peak of Mount Hermon.

שיר-שבח לעוטי זיו הפנים

בַּעֲנָוָה אֲנִי נִרְכָּן אֶל מוּל הֲדַר קִמְטֵי פְּנֵיכֶם
חוֹלְמֵי יְרוּשָׁלַיִם
לַחְגֹּג אֶת פֶּלֶא תְּקוּמַת זִכְרְכֶם בְּקִרְבִּי.
מֵנֶץ בִּי שִׁמְכֶם כְּמַטֶּה שֶׁעָלָה פִּתְאוֹם פּוֹרֵחַ.
רַבִּי דָּוִד חָסִין וְסִימָנְךָ ט׳ בָּנוֹת
כֻּלָּן עוֹלוֹת בָּאֳהָלוֹת.
וְאַתְּ פִּרְחָה בַּת יוֹסֵף
כְּלֵךְ כַּלָּה בְּהִינוּמָה
תּוֹפֶפֶת שׁוּרוֹת הַשִּׁיר
כְּמוֹ בְּאֶצְעֲדוֹת הַכֶּסֶף.
וְאַתָּה שְׁלֹמֹה גּוֹזְלָן
וּמַרְכֹּלֶת שִׁירָתְךָ עַל אֵם דְּרָכִים
צֳרִי וְקִנָּמוֹן וְכָל רָאשֵׁי בְשָׂמִים.
וְגַם אֲנִי אֶעֱנֶה לָכֶם שִׁיר
מֵרֹאשׁ אֲמָנָה וּמֵרֹאשׁ שְׂנִיר.
מִמְּנַת יוֹמִי וּמִקֶּצֶף חַיַּי
לְהָקִים לָכֶם קֵן שֶׁל קֶבַע בְּתוֹכִי

To Speak of a City to Its Face

Ah, my Jews driven out from a city
whose roads slope downward
pushing at their feet to leave.
Ah, my Jews driven out from a city
that sealed its name on their backs
like a flickering sign in the universe.
Toledo.

לדבר על עיר בפניה

אַהּ, יְהוּדֵי הַנֶּעֱזָבִים מֵעִיר
שֶׁרְחוֹבוֹתֶיהָ מוֹרָדוֹת מוֹרָדוֹת
דּוֹחֲקִים בְּרַגְלֵיהֶם לָצֵאת.
אַהּ, יְהוּדֵי הַנֶּעֱזָבִים מֵעִיר
אֲשֶׁר חָתְמָה בְּגַבָּם אֶת שְׁמָהּ
כְּמוֹ אוֹת מְהַבְהֵב בָּעוֹלָם.
טוֹלֵדוֹ.

My Mother Collects Down[64]

When Father was upset
he would stick his finger in his mouth
and write on the wall:
Nak bekesrut shanim
lah huppa, lah banim.[65]
And my mother keeps collecting down
from every stall in the souk
and from every nook,
calling: Assidi Massoud,[66]
some nice ivory for my son,
some burnished brass for the happiness of my eldest.
And the women call after her to hearten:
Akbal endek akbal endek Allala Simcha.[67]
And already in the closets ivory upon ivory
and in the drawers brass upon brass,
and I say to her: Chli ayima,[68]
my spread sheet burns in the sun
and my huppa[69] is the huppa of crows.

---

[64]Following a custom whereby the parents of the groom provide the bride with down blankets, beddings, and other gifts in a pre-wedding ceremony.

[65]Arabic: Your legacy will be brief / no huppa, no progeny.

[66]Arabic: Mister Massoud

[67]Arabic: Soon in your house, soon in your house, Madam Simcha. [Namely: We'll soon be dancing in your son's wedding.]

[68]Don't bother, Mother.

[69]The huppa (wedding) canopy is usually a sheet.

אמי אוגרת פוך

כְּשֶׁאַבָּא הָיָה רוֹגֵז
הָיָה שָׂם אֶצְבַּע בַּפֶּה וְרוֹשֵׁם בַּקִּיר:
נָאק בְּקֶסְרוּט שָׁנִים (הִנְּךָ לְקִצּוּר שָׁנִים)
לָא חֶפָּה, לָא בָּנִים (בְּלִי חֻפָּה, בְּלִי בָּנִים).
אִמִּי אוֹגֶרֶת פּוּךְ
מִכָּל דּוּכָן שֶׁבַּשּׁוּק
וּמִכָּל כּוּךְ
וְקוֹרֵאת: אַסִּידִי מַסְעוּד (אֲדוֹנִי מַסְעוּד),
אֵיזֶה שֶׁנְהָב יָפֶה לִבְנִי
אֵיזוֹ נְחֹשֶׁת קָלָל לְשִׂמְחַת בְּכוֹרִי.
וְהַנָּשִׁים בְּעִקְבוֹתֶיהָ מְלַבּוֹת:
עָקְבַּאל עֶנְדֶאק אַלַּלָּה שִׂמְחָה
(בְּקָרוֹב אֶצְלֵךְ בְּקָרוֹב אֶצְלֵךְ גְּבֶרֶת שִׂמְחָה)
וְהָאֲרוֹנוֹת כְּבָר שֶׁנְהָב עַל שֶׁנְהָב
וְהַשִּׁדּוֹת קָלָל עַל קָלָל.
וַאֲנִי אוֹמֵר לָהּ:
כְּלִי אַיִמָּה (עִזְבִי אִמָּא),
סָדִין שֶׁלִּי פָּרוּשׂ צָרוּב בַּשֶּׁמֶשׁ
וְחֻפָּתִי חֻפַּת עוֹרְבִים.

Scaffolding

On the threshold of half a house in the Land of Israel
my father stood
pointing to the sides and saying:
Upon these ruins
one day we will build a kitchen
to cook in it a Leviathan's tail
and a wild bull,[70]
upon these ruins
we will build a corner for prayer
to make room
for a bit of holiness.
My father remained on the threshold
and I, my entire life,
have been erecting scaffolding
reaching up to the sky.

---

[70]The Leviathan and the wild bull, both legendary, are promised to the righteous in the hereafter.

פיגומים

עַל סַף חֲצִי בַּיִת בְּאֶרֶץ יִשְׂרָאֵל
עָמַד אָבִי
מַצְבִּיעַ לִצְדָדִים וְאוֹמֵר:
בַּהֲרִיסוֹת הָאֵלֶּה
נִבְנֶה פַּעַם מִטְבָּח
לְבַשֵּׁל בּוֹ זְנַב לִוְיָתָן
וְשׁוֹר הַבָּר,
וּבַהֲרִיסוֹת הָאֵלֶּה
נָקִים פִּנַּת תְּפִלָּה
לִמְצֹא מָקוֹם
לְמִקְדָּשׁ מְעַט.
אָבִי נִשְׁאַר בַּסַּף
וַאֲנִי כָּל יָמַי
מַצִּיב פִּגּוּמִים
אֶל לֵב הַשָּׁמַיִם.

Acknowledgments

The following poems have appeared in the following publications:

Asymptote: "Elegies for ben Shushan";
Guernica: "My Father Gave the Neighbors";
Modern Poetry in Translation: "When I Was a Child of Light," "With the Kids," "Zohra El Fassia," "Al-Keskas ul-Ferran";
Plume: "Uncle Yehuda Sharvit Between Marrakesh and Draa";
Poetry International Rotterdam: "Becoming a Weaver," "We Are Strangers," "Heart Valve";
Poetry Magazine: "Scaffolding."

The poems in this collection were previously published in Hebrew by Hakibbutz Hameuchad in *Blindfolded Landscapes* (2013) and *Timbisert, A Moroccan Bird—New and Selected Poems* (2009).

I would like to express my deepest gratitude to Rachel Calahorra Bitton for her invaluable professional assistance to me throughout this project.

About the Author

The recipient of the 2015 Israel Prize in Literature, Erez Bitton was born in 1942 to Moroccan parents in Oran, Algeria, and immigrated to Israel in 1948. Blinded by a stray hand grenade he found near his home in Lod, he spent the rest of his childhood in Jerusalem's School for the Blind. He received a B.A. in social work from The Hebrew University of Jerusalem, and an M.A. in psychology from Bar Ilan University. He wrote a weekly column for the Israeli daily *Ma'ariv* and worked as a social worker and as a psychologist. His first two books, *A Moroccan Offering* (1976) and *The Book of Na'na* (1979), established him as the founding father of Mizrahi poetry in Israel—the first poet to take on the conflict between North African immigrants and the Ashkenazi society, and the first to use Judeo-Arabic dialect in his poetry. The author of five poetry collections and a play, he has served as chairman of the Hebrew Writers Association, and is the Editor in Chief of the literary journal *Apyrion*, which he founded in 1982. Among his awards are the Miriam Talpir Prize (1982), the Prime Minister Award (1988), the Yehuda Amichai Award (2014), the Bialik Lifetime Achievement Award (2014), as well as the 2015 American Sephardi Federation Lifetime Achievement Award. Bitton lives in Tel Aviv with his wife Rachel Calahorra Bitton, and is father to a son and a daughter.

Books Published in Hebrew

A Moroccan Offering (poetry), Eked, 1976 [*Mincha Maroka'it*]
The Book of Na'na (poetry), Eked, 1979 [*Sefer Ha-Nana*]
Intercontinental Bird (poetry), Hakibbutz Hameuchad, 1990 [*Tzipor Bein Yabashot*]
Soulica (play), Snir, 2005 [*Sullika*]

Timbisert, A Moroccan Bird (poetry), Hakibbutz Hameuchad, 2009 [*Timbisert, Tzipor Maroca'it*]
Blindfolded Landscapes (poetry), Hakibbutz Hameuchad, 2013 [*Nofim Chavushei Einayim*]

Books in Translation

The Book of Na'na – French: Editions Saint Germain, Paris, 1981

About the Translator

Tsipi Keller was born in Prague, raised in Israel, and has been living in the U.S. since 1974. The author of ten books, she is the recipient of several literary awards, including National Endowment for the Arts Translation Fellowships, New York Foundation for the Arts fiction grants, and an Armand G. Erpf award from Columbia University. Her most recent translation collections are *Poets on the Edge: An Anthology of Contemporary Hebrew Poetry* (SUNY Press); *The Hymns of Job & Other Poems*, a Lannan Translation Selection (BOA Editions); and *Reality Crumbs* (SUNY Press).

About Eli Hirsch

Eli Hirsch is a poet, editor, and literary critic. Born in Petach Tikva in 1962, he published his first poems in 1979, and holds a graduate degree in Philosophy from Tel Aviv University. He is the author of four volumes of poetry, and his most recent collection is *Hanging Gardens of Tel Aviv* (Hakibbutz Hameuchad, 2012). He has published numerous book reviews and essays, and, since 2007, writes a weekly column on poetry in the Literary Supplement of the daily *Yediot Ahronot.* He was Editor in Chief at Modan Publishing, and is currently (since 2003) the Literary Editor at Hargol Publishing House. Hirsch teaches Creative Writing in the Literature Department at Tel Aviv University.

The Lannan Translations Selection Series

Ljuba Merlina Bortolani, *The Siege*
Olga Orozco, *Engravings Torn from Insomnia*
Gérard Martin, *The Hiddenness of the World*
Fadhil Al-Azzawi, *Miracle Maker*
Sándor Csoóri, *Before and After the Fall: New Poems*
Francisca Aguirre, *Ithaca*
Jean-Michel Maulpoix, *A Matter of Blue*
Willow, Wine, Mirror, Moon: Women's Poems from Tang China
Felipe Benítez Reyes, *Probable Lives*
Ko Un, *Flowers of a Moment*
Paulo Henriques Britto, *The Clean Shirt of It*
Moikom Zeqo, *I Don't Believe in Ghosts*
Adonis (Ali Ahmad Sa'id), *Mihyar of Damascus, His Songs*
Maya Bejerano, *The Hymns of Job and Other Poems*
Novica Tadić, *Dark Things*
Praises & Offenses: Three Women Poets of the Dominican Republic
Ece Temelkuran, *Book of the Edge*
Aleš Šteger, *The Book of Things*
Nikola Madzirov, *Remnants of Another Age*
Carsten René Nielsen, *House Inspections*
Jacek Gutorow, *The Folding Star and Other Poems*
Marosa di Giorgio, *Diadem*
Zeeshan Sahil, *Light and Heavy Things*
Sohrab Sepehri, *The Oasis of Now*
Dariusz Sośnicki, *The World Shared: Poems*
Nguyen Phan Que Mai, *The Secret of Hoa Sen*
Aleš Debeljak, *Smugglers*
Erez Bitton, *You Who Cross My Path*

For more on the Lannan Translations Selection Series
visit our website:
www.boaeditions.org